A PLACE TO STAY

30 EXTRAORDINARY HOTELS

A PLACE TO STAY

30 EXTRAORDINARY HOTELS

PHOTOGRAPHY Grant Sheehan
TEXT Shelley-Maree Cassidy

conran
OCTOPUS

ACKNOWLEDGEMENTS

Much thanks is due to Robert Achten, Crispin Bassett, Katrina Bennett, Stefano Bigatti, Silvia Biaggi, Jean-Pierre & Elaine Bourbeillon, Wendy Cameron, Liz Cathie, Scott Cato, Shashi Bashi & Bina Chaddha, Jane Connor, David Cowdrey, Donna Cross, Caroline Cundall, Scott Kennedy, Suha Ersov, Elizabeth Robertson, Lauren Robertson, Richard Weston... and the swimming man in the Perivolas pool.

First published in 2000 by
Conran Octopus Limited
2–4 Heron Quays
London E14 4JP
This edition published in 2001

ISBN 1 84091 150 6

First published by Phantom House Books in 1999

Designed by Origin Design

British Library Cataloguing-in-Publication Data
A catalogue record for this book is available from the British Library

Printed in China

CONTENTS

A PLACE TO STAY

YOUR TRAVEL LIFE HAS THE ESSENCE OF A DREAM. IT IS SOMETHING OUTSIDE THE NORMAL, YET YOU ARE IN IT. IT IS PEOPLED WITH CHARACTERS YOU HAVE NEVER SEEN BEFORE AND IN ALL PROBABILITY WILL NEVER SEE AGAIN. IT BRINGS OCCASIONAL HOMESICKNESS, AND LONELINESS AND PANGS OF LONGING... BUT YOU ARE LIKE THE VIKINGS OR THE MASTER MARINERS OF THE ELIZABETHAN AGE, WHO HAVE GONE INTO THE WORLD OF ADVENTURE, AND HOME IS NOT HOME UNTIL YOU RETURN. Agatha Christie

This book is essentially about homes away from home for the traveller, about places to stay – the accommodation and the destinations. Hotels have always played a major part in travel, whether the purpose is business or pleasure. Often scenes of great events, mystery, intrigue and romance are contained within their walls, as may be history, both individual and international. The hotels featured here all distinguish themselves as fascinating places to stay, although each is as disparate and distinct as its guests.

In the era of the 747 no journey is so long that it is still much of an adventure reaching your destination. Negotiating airports and fellow passengers are often the most arduous elements. A click of the mouse now brings instant virtual access to the world and its cultures; actually being there seems to matter less and less. So, does travel still serve to broaden the mind? The desire to see for oneself is unchecked. More and more people are travelling, and tourism is the leading global industry.

THE USE OF TRAVELLING IS TO REGULATE IMAGINATION BY REALITY, AND INSTEAD OF THINKING HOW THINGS MAY BE, TO SEE THEM AS THEY ARE. Samuel Johnson

Even in this age of instant information transfer, travelling involves mundane process – booking tickets, packing and labelling luggage, and obtaining travel documents. The journey itself may be a smooth uncomplicated passage, or one with frustrating delays, bad service, lost luggage and expensive transfers. It is with a sense of relief that the traveller arrives at their destination. You reach your hotel, and whether modest or grand, old or new, it will serve as your temporary home away from home.

On entering the hotel, it is the reception that makes the first impression. You are checked in, presented with your key and shown to your room. And so begins the experience, good or otherwise, that puts the stamp on your stay. The refuge of the hotel room, a cocoon to cosset the travel-weary. Does your room offer a view, is it quiet, the bed comfortable, the bathroom well fitted out? These walls enclose much of your travelling experience, and become your retreat from the unfamiliar world beyond, a private space where you can rest and regroup, free from observation and domestic responsibilities. Is it any wonder we expect so much of our hotel room?

The public rooms are the outer sanctum, the transitory spaces where encounters are limited, privacy may be respected but our need of company, sustenance and service is met. It is here that we expect the hotel to wrap its arms around its guests, providing a world that is enclosed but not entirely exclusive.

TRAVELLING GIVES ONE SOMETHING TO TALK ABOUT WHEN ONE GETS HOME... AND THE SUBJECTS OF CONVERSATION ARE NOT SO NUMEROUS THAT ONE CAN NEGLECT AN OPPORTUNITY OF ADDING TO ONE'S STORE. Aldous Huxley

Of course the truly great hotels go a step further. While they provide the care and comfort we hope for, they offer that extra quality not always realised for the most hopeful of travellers – a memorable experience. These are the hotels that go the greater distance, that have a special quality much sought after but finally matchless – their very own sense of style. Our aim has been to capture that elusive quality in this book.

The hotels shown here are an arbitrary and personal selection, chosen on the basis of their style and interest, not tariff. Others we would have liked to include were ruled out by space or time constraints. Still more are opening as this book goes to print. Other travellers have recommended their own favourites. Maybe another book, another time...

We invite you to indulge in the most enjoyable of travelling experiences – to vicariously venture into a variety of hotels and to visit some of the most interesting destinations. Whether it's the ultimate urban experience of New York, the unavoidably cool attitude of the Ice Hotel in Swedish Lapland, the geographical hotchpotch of Las Vegas, the serene Lake Palace Hotel in Udaipur or the sanctuary of Kyoto's Tawaraya Inn – 'bookmark' your choices for your next real, or virtual, journey. Bon voyage!

FOR EVERY TRAVELLER WHO HAS ANY TASTE OF HIS OWN, THE ONLY USEFUL GUIDEBOOK WILL BE THE ONE WHICH HE HIMSELF HAS WRITTEN... THE ONLY SATISFACTORY SUBSTITUTE FOR A GUIDE WRITTEN BY ONESELF IS A GUIDE WHICH IS COPIOUSLY ILLUSTRATED. TO KNOW THE IMAGES OF THINGS IS THE NEXT BEST TO KNOWING THE THINGS THEMSELVES... Aldous Huxley: Along the Road

The Ambassade Hotel stretches along the Herengracht

AMBASSADE HOTEL | Amsterdam | The Netherlands

ON THE WATERFRONT

In what is one of the world's great cities on water, the Hotel Ambassade is canal-side, a priority in choosing a place to stay in Amsterdam. Situated in the historical centre of Amsterdam on the Herengracht (Gentleman's Canal) the hotel has a peaceful setting slightly off the major tourist track. Yet it is close to good cafés, restaurants and bookshops, to the many museums, the floating flower market and shopping streets. Nearby is the tree-lined Jordaan area, an old neighbourhood undergoing a renovation renaissance, and on almost every street there seems to be an Indonesian restaurant, reflecting the legacy of Dutch explorers and spice traders who journeyed back and forth to what was once called New Holland.

The Ambassade is a row of gabled centuries-old canal houses. On a charmingly small scale, the ten buildings are cobbled together as a hotel. Each is four or five storeys high, with steep staircases, twisting corridors, and low beamed ceilings. No designer drew this hotel up: it has evolved in its own eccentric way. The Ambassade has a literary tradition, reflected in names signed in the visitor's book. The hotel is apparently favoured by writers such as Oliver Sacks, Salman Rushdie and John Le Carré. No doubt many were on book promoting gigs in the city. There is soon to be a hotel library, to house the many books signed by the author guests.

The hotel is discreetly signed, and blends well into the essentially residential area. Despite being made up of ten houses, it is comparatively small, with none of its fifty-two rooms alike. This is an elegant individual and friendly hotel. The ornate breakfast room overlooking the canal serves a generous traditional Dutch repast. Because it is such a pleasant and spacious room, with white lacquered walls and two-storey high windows, it is better to forgo room service and eat here. The antique-filled sitting room next door is a good location to enjoy a leisurely mid-morning coffee or an afternoon drink, admiring the old and ornate walnut clock with its moving fleet of ships.

Our room looked out over the canal. The large windows opened wide on the early autumn afternoon, letting in the still warm sun. Just above the street and heads of passers-by, the room had a gracious and welcoming feel, the atmosphere of a comfortable home. The bed was placed in an alcove, with table and chairs placed beside the window, adding to the impression of being in a living room. With a glass of wine and food bought from a nearby café, we sat and watched Amsterdam go by. The boat traffic along the canal is a reminder that this is a maritime city and major port. There was also a constant stream of cars and bicycles, and the sound of murmuring Amsterdammers headed for cafés, to visit friends, or going home...

At night, the city's bridges, illuminated by tiny lights placed around their arches, seem suspended over a void until a boat comes by with its lights on. The huge variety of boats range from the trim to the wallowing-noisy tourist craft, a wooden dinghy being rowed to a nearby restaurant, barges motoring by on business, homes afloat and vessels tied up by their owners who are refuelling at a convenient café...

The Ambassade's added water attraction is a massage centre with flotation tanks. It provides a pleasant remedy for stress and jetlag, and perhaps writer's block.

Think of an archery target and you have a bead on Amsterdam, laid out within concentric circles formed by its five main canals. The web of smaller waterways within brings the total number to a hundred and sixty canals, the city claiming to have more canals than Venice. Traversing these watery barriers are 1,281 bridges, negotiated by 550,000 bicycles, and even more cars.

Hiring a bike is an option if you prefer your own wheels, but Amsterdam is a city to enjoy on foot. At night, uncurtained interiors offer glimpses of how the citizens live, contemporary versions of Vermeer's light-infused canvasses which captured everyday Dutch scenes in the seventeenth century.

Cruising the grand canals in a rented motorboat is a rather more elegant alternative to a two-seater water bike. Tourist boats provide a seaman's perspective on houses built along the canal banks by wealthy mariners during the prosperous age of merchant sail. Famed for museums focused on art – Van Gogh, the Rijksmuseum with its Rembrandts and Vermeers and the modern art of the Stedelijk – Amsterdam also caters to more down-to-earth tastes with museums specialising in subjects as diverse as trams, beer, sex and football. Something for everyone...

Original beams in Attic bedroom number 68

The Gable of the first house of the Ambassade's ten

The Café 'T Smalle, a short stroll or sail from the hotel

The modern and the medieval coexist comfortably in this very cosmopolitan city. Fans of architecture should see the quirky apartment complex of Eigen Haard (Our Hearth), on Michel de Klerk's drawing board from 1913 to 1920. The striking Science Centre New Metropolis by Renzo Piano rises like an ocean liner from the harbour and there is cutting-edge design from the appropriately named radical Dutch architect Rem Koolhaas. Check out Architectura & Natura, a specialist bookshop at Leliegracht 44, for guidebooks on modern Dutch buildings.

Amsterdam has a four hundred-year association with diamonds. It is also linked with tulips, which have their own fascinating history. As the Hotel Ambassade has a connection with writers, it seems fitting to mention two excellent books featuring tulips, one a novel, the other a history.

TULIP FEVER, BY DEBORAH MOGGACH (PUBLISHED BY HEINEMANN)

The Amsterdam of the early seventeenth century was immortalised in seemingly serene domestic interiors painted by Vermeer and Rembrandt. Moggach's book adds another dimension to the artists' canvases. Set in 1630s Amsterdam, a typical renaissance love triangle draws a wealthy elderly merchant, his beautiful but frustrated young wife, and the painter commissioned to paint the couple's portrait. The artist becomes entangled in a series of emotional and financial speculations, including tulip-bulb trading, and the lives of the three central characters are utterly changed. The text is interspersed with sixteen beautifully reproduced Dutch paintings, a novel addition to this work of fiction.

THE TULIP: THE STORY OF A FLOWER THAT HAS MADE MEN MAD; BY ANNA PAVORD: (PUBLISHED BY BLOOMSBURY, APPROPRIATELY)

A gardening writer, Pavord has recorded the bizarre history of the tulip in a massive book that is both scholarly and entertaining. Originating in Central Asia, tulips were transported to Europe by the Turks. In the 1730s the Dutch were overtaken by 'tulipomania', with single bulbs changing hands for the price of a house. Other countries including France caught the tulip fever. While the Europeans eventually regained their composure, the tulip's popularity now reaches out to embrace the New World. Pavord's book is illustrated with hundreds of full page prints of the stylish flower.

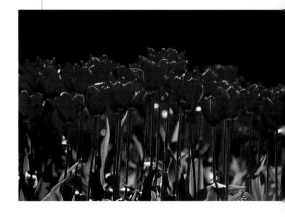

The Ambassade Hotel	Telephone: +31 20 626 2333
Herengracht 341	Facsimile: +31 20 6245321
1016 Az Amsterdam	Email: info@ambassade-hotel.nl
THE NETHERLANDS	Internet: www.ambassade-hotel.nl

FORTRESS FRANCE

Château de Bagnols does not fit the fairy-tale version of a traditional wedding-cake style castle. This is a fortress to be taken seriously, a vantage point built in the early thirteenth century to forewarn defenders of approaching enemy.

Conceived in the age of chivalry, the fortress may have a new vocation as a hotel, but it upholds the medieval tradition of hospitality toward visitors. Guests are welcomed through its portcullis, their transport tethered and tended to in the car park, rather than the former stables, converted as part of the accommodation adjoining the Château.

With towers, moat and a drawbridge entrance, the Château de Bagnols is a triumph of restoration over ruin. Originally built in 1221 it is now one of the historic treasures of France. But it was left to moulder after the Revolution, and a decade ago it was a sadly neglected ruin, with leaking roofs, cracked walls, a home to a family of crows and surrounded by a wilderness garden.

Prince Charming may have come late but the fortress has been awakened from its long sleep to again become the great property it once was.

Traces of the avenues and bassins marking the axis of the old garden were uncovered in the overgrown orchard, enclosed by a stone wall punctuated with small round decorative towers. An avenue of limes follows the terrace walls and four parterres, planted with cherry trees, are sheltered by yew hedges. The restored grounds recreate the original gardens, which, like the Château, overlook the little medieval village of Bagnols and the hills beyond.

CHÂTEAU DE BAGNOLS | Bagnols | France

View of the Château from the garden

A contemporary touch is the glass wall that allows a view of the sleek courtyard kitchen where regional specialities are prepared. The Beaujolais style of cuisine has been described by Elizabeth David as 'the most sumptuous kind of country cooking brought to a point of finesse, beyond which it would lose its character.'

Many meet for coffee or aperitifs in the Grand Salon, where they are spoiled for viewing choice: splendid wall paintings or large windows offering views over the countryside and into the courtyard. When we visited, the room was decorated with massive bowls of peony roses, out of season at that time of the year. The elaborately carved Renaissance fireplace dominates the room, and at each side of the hearth, doors lead to tower rooms.

Staying here is well worth the expense, and the privacy and shelter found behind the castle walls have appealed to many wearied by fame. The Château is peaceful and perfect without being pretentious. Sitting on the terrace looking out over the gardens to the hills and valleys beyond is to be lord of all you survey, which one guest, Charles VIII of France, assuredly was. The King's visit in 1490 is commemorated by the royal coat of arms above the dining room's Gothic fireplace.

The hotel's twenty rooms and suites have been expertly restored and each has a different character. Antique beds are hung with period silk velvets and embroideries, and dressed with pure linen embroidered sheets fit for modern-day royalty.

Preserved within the Château's massive walls are a series of striking wall paintings, examples of embellishments added in times of peace and prosperity. The earliest date from the fifteenth century. Many were hidden behind partitions, plasterwork and other modifications made over time, and were only discovered during recent restoration work.

The Château exudes history and grandeur, but these qualities never overwhelm the aura of comfort and sense of human scale. Its bucolic setting, the Beaujolais region in the east of France, has been compared with Tuscany. This though, is quieter and less visited. Rolling green hills are blanketed with forest and vineyard, and hilltop villages, picturesque châteaux, fine churches and farm buildings are constructed of the local honey-coloured stone known as *pierre dorée* (golden stone).

The Grand Salon with its Renaissance fireplace

The Bedroom of the Guichard D'Oingt suite

In the weeks of autumn, the vine leaves turn colour and the grape harvest is brought in at the famous vineyards that make up the Beaujolais wine trail. The fruit is picked by hand in the vineyards such as Fleurie, Julienas and St-Amour; and the wines are drunk – with others produced by neighbouring Burgundy and Rhone – at the Château and restaurants in the surrounding towns which include St-Paule and Villefranche.

A head start on decorating a more modest castle can be made in the Château's boutique shop, where customers may be tempted by a collection of more than 500 specially designed items. This stock includes handblown French glasses inspired by an eighteenth-century Burgundian design, furniture, silverware and Limoges porcelain. The charming pink and white uniforms of the housemaids are not for sale.

The Beaujolais countryside viewed from the terrace

The Château is open from April to January, and would provide a great retreat for Christmas. Arrangements can be made with the management to open during the closed season, should you wish to have a castle to yourself.

How to get there: Travel by fast train (TGV) from Paris to Lyons, and then by car to Bagnols; otherwise fly to Lyons or drive down from Paris.

Château de Bagnols	Telephone: +33 4 7471 4000
69620 Bagnols-en-Beaujolais	Facsimile: +33 4 7471 4049
FRANCE	Internet: www.bagnols.com

An old cart from bygone Bagnols days.

The Hotel Claris

THE HOTEL CLARIS | Barcelona | Spain

'A BALANCED DYNAMIC'

On Spain's Costa Dorada, named for its golden sand beaches, is the Mediterranean seaport of Barcelona, the capital city of the Catalonian region.

Catalonia has a long and proud history of rebellion and independence. It was from here that Christopher Columbus set out on his voyage of discovery. Today it is deservedly famous for its collection of extraordinary buildings designed by Spain's most famous architect, Antoni Gaudí, during the early part of the twentieth century, as well as architecture from the fifteenth century.

Even the airport is stylish, a fitting entry to this design-oriented city, which mixes medieval, Art Nouveau and modern architecture, and was home to great artists such as Pablo Picasso, Salvador Dalí and Joan Miró.

Behind the ornate nineteenth-century façade of the Hotel Claris is yet another collection in this city of collections. The Claris has its own Egyptian museum on the mezzanine above the lobby, open only to guests. Here you can take tea and out-stare a small sphinx, inspect the mummies, statues and carvings and pretend to be a discovering archaeologist, all in the comfort of your own hotel.

The owner of the hotel has assembled this ancient collection. Senor Jordi Clos i Llombart is one of Spain's leading Egyptologists and the founder of Barcelona's Egyptology Museum, which houses the rest of his collection.

Behind the exterior of what was once a palace are cutting edge interiors, balancing classicism and contemporary design, typical of Barcelona.

The Claris has an expansive lobby in which guests may watch the world go by. Here, ancient mosaic fragments and marble toga-clad Roman busts are juxtaposed with contemporary furniture by Oscar Tusquets. The hotel doorman, clad in white, is another chic trademark of the Claris.

Our room is reminiscent of a ship's cabin, and had parquet floors, kilim rugs and intriguing antique pieces, modern furniture and relics. But few sailors would be used to rich colours of russet wood and purple and room to move on two levels, all of which make this such a stylish space. And the closest expanse of water is the generously sized open-air swimming pool up on the hotel roof, where a city centre panoramic view is a bonus.

Hotel Claris is in the heart of metropolitan Barcelona, only a street away from the most fashionable and gracious avenue in the city, the Paseo de Gracia. On this broad and tree-lined street are two of Gaudí's most admired and visited buildings – the Casa Batlló, and the Casa Milá (known as La Pedrera, the Quarry). It is worth the climb up to the Casa Milá's amazing roof, topped with giant surreal superstructures – chimneys and ventilation shafts said to have inspired Darth Vader's helmet!

These are but two of Gaudí's bizarre and brilliant buildings, which are often likened to massive sculptures. While highly original, his forms are functional – the free form architecture reflecting his belief in providing natural methods of ventilation. Curved lines in the interiors, incorporation of the outdoors, and living spaces with movable walls are trademarks of this creative architect's unique work. Now recognised as a visionary, Gaudí's ideas are compatible with modern architectural thought and the growing acceptance of the benefits of 'biological living'.

A mecca for admirers of Modernism, Barcelona has Europe's greatest collection of Art Nouveau buildings. Although the movement inspired him, Gaudí's interpretation was unique. A soaring sight on the city skyline is the spectacular sandcastle spires of his Church of the Sagrada Familia. Only one filigree stone tower was complete when Gaudí died in 1926 but work continues, a hundred years since it was begun, on this evolving organic artwork. In the manner of the great medieval cathedrals, his church is still not finished.

After marvelling at the Gaudí buildings close to the Claris, sit at the bar of the nearby Replay café, drink coffee, and watch the parade of passing Barcelonans. Or visit the design store of Vincón, with everything stylish for the home from fabrics to furniture.

Barcelona's most famous street, La Rambla, is an amble from the Paseo de Gracia. The busy promenade leading down to the waterfront is edged with cafés and bars, dotted with seats, trees and newsstands. Its mass of flower stalls colour and perfume the length of the street. La Rambla continues to the Columbus monument honouring the Catalan discoverer of the New World.

Roof top pool at the Claris

Storefront on the Rambla Avenue

Barcelona is considered Spain's culinary capital, and it's here you will find one of the most spectacular food markets. Mercat de la Boqueria has been the central market in the Rambla area for more than a hundred and sixty years. Ornate iron columns, buttresses and arches support a large covered pavilion, underneath which are the five hundred or so food stalls. Few of the market's original Art Nouveau stalls and fittings are left, the most famous is Ramona's. With its bright stained-glass signs, cast iron columns and mosaic tiled sides, it attracts many admirers.

A *xuxo*, a fluffy cream-filled type of croissant sprinkled with sugar, is a delicious breakfast. You can walk the damage off, checking out the cheeses, wines, meats and fish. By now you may be ready to try a tortilla while appraising mushrooms, olives, herbs, salad greens... Then take a rest from this gastronomic onslaught at one of the tapas bars, with a glass of cava, the Catalan sparkling wine.

Another of Barcelona's treasured collections is the paintings of Picasso. The Museu Picasso is in the medieval Barri Gòtic (Gothic Quarter), with its warren of streets and plazas one of the city's most interesting neighbourhoods.

The Casa Batlló, façade designed by Antoni Gaudí in 1904, with its 'dragon-back' roof of green ceramic tile

Luckily, to enjoy all this and more, the days seem to last longer. That may be because meals are later – lunch between 1 to 3pm, dinner around 9 or 10pm. The late nights can be spent in the many designer bars and clubs.

For a restful daytime experience, spend time in the gardens of the Park Güell. Take a picnic, sit on the mosaic tiled benches on the great serpentine curving terrace and admire the ornamented pavilions of another inventive and original Gaudí legacy to this fortunate city.

Hotel Claris Pau Claris 150 08009 Barcelona SPAIN	Telephone +34 3 487 62 62
	Facsimile +34 3 487 54 43

The Marlborough Sounds

HOTEL D'URVILLE   Blenheim   New Zealand

NEW VINTAGE

At the top of the South Island of New Zealand lie the sheltered blue waters of the spectacular Marlborough Sounds. This marine playground provides a perfect environment for water sports from sailing and cruising, to diving and sea kayaking. The myriad of peaceful bays and coves that make up the Sounds are home to blue dolphins, penguins, seals and native birds.

The Hotel d'Urville

Not far from this water haven is the Hotel d'Urville. With its grand-columned frontage, this is a landmark building in the small town of Blenheim, centre of the 'new world' wine region of Marlborough. The hotel is named after renowned French explorer Dumont d'Urville, a brilliant enigmatic sailor who made two great voyages to the Pacific as Commander of the ship Astrolabe in the 1800s. In search of a site for a French penal colony, he surveyed New Zealand, and charted the fjords of the Sounds, but was beaten by Britain to claiming the country for France.

However, two hundred years later, there is a far more favourable connection with France than a prison would have been: French wine stock grows here, and Marlborough sauvignon blancs, such as the famous Cloudy Bay label, win awards and accolades in Europe and America.

The bank vault lobby

This is one of the key viticultural regions of New Zealand, where the climate has been compared to Burgundy in France. Yet New Zealand's long narrow shape, which means that nowhere is more than eighty miles from the sea, provides a unique maritime climate. Most of the vineyards are in coastal areas, warmed by day with clear sunlight and cooled by sea breezes at night.

In only thirty years since the first vineyard was established, Marlborough has become the largest wine-growing region in New Zealand. Some thirty or so wineries have been established, growing grape varieties such as Sauvignon Blanc, Chardonnay, Riesling, and Pinot Gris. Red varieties such as Pinot Noir, Cabernet Sauvignon and Merlot are also planted here. The soil types, abundant sunshine, long autumns and crisp cool winters have proved the right ingredients to deliver world class wines. Such is the quality of the terroir here that international wine companies have invested in the region, with Swiss, French and Australian labels staking out their own claims.

Built in the 1920s, the old bank building has been skilfully converted into a new use. The grand staircase leads guests upstairs to what was once a walk-in vault, and which now forms the central corridor that leads to the bedrooms. Now you can deposit yourself for safe keeping in this small nine-room hotel. The huge steel vault doors have been kept, complete with their original brass plaques and studs.

Whilst the decoration is eclectic, this is not a euphemism for a mess. Themed rooms are a trend in many hotels, as proprietors strive to differentiate their establishment from others to appeal to the often-jaded palette of the regular traveller bored with the standard hotel room look. The themes here are understated, often more of a hint rather than fully realised, which is a more elegant interpretation.

The classic lines of the d'Urville Suite recall New Zealand's
colonial days, with a nautical feel in the blue panelling to the
dado line, a brass ship's bell, charts and antique maps. Drawings
by the Astrolabe's resident artist line the walls.

A blaze of warm red enlivens the entrance to the Colours Room. Bold contrasts of high impact colours on the walls and fabrics are picked up by glass ornaments. This is a high-energy room with a relaxing atmosphere.

Downstairs is the d'Urville wine bar and brasserie, with its much praised menu and a young chef who uses the local produce and wines to full advantage, gaining the restaurant an international reputation. A patchwork of orchards and vineyards, Marlborough is described as New Zealand's gourmet's province, and is home to the famous green-lipped mussels, farmed salmon and locally grown olive oil. During the long hot summer, guests can sit at tables in the open air surrounded by vines. And in winter, sampling the regional red wines in front of the fire in the bar is a welcome relaxation after a day on the slopes of the nearby skifields.

With its agreeable (more than agreeable actually) climate, the country's highest sunshine hours and an easy going lifestyle focused on wine, food and water, Marlborough is a tourist magnet. And the whale-watching capital of the world, Kaikoura, is less than two hours drive away for the biggest fish story of them all.

THIS REGION WAS CERTAINLY
THE ONE THAT GOT AWAY FROM THE FRENCH!

The Kuba room is adorned with old African
ceremonial textiles and tapestries.
An old teak box displays small intricate carvings,
and colourful telephone wire baskets made by
Ndebele women.

How to get there: Fly to Wellington, then on to Blenheim, or by
ferry from Wellington. For detailed information on New Zealand wines,
visit www.nzwine.com

Hotel d'Urville	Telephone: +64 3 577 9945
27 Queen Street	
Blenheim	Facsimile: +64 3 577 9946
NEW ZEALAND	Internet: www.nzcom.co.nz/travel/durville

BLISS AT BLUMAU... RESTORATION OASIS

We appear to be lost. Our taxi driver has slowed and is anxiously leaning forward to scan passing road signs. We can see his worried face reflected in the rear view mirror. Our destination is the Rogner-Bad Blumau; a spa hotel located one hour's drive south of Vienna. It is nearly dusk, and our one-hour journey is in danger of taking two as we drive through yet another picturesque village – or maybe it's the same one – in the lush green Austrian countryside.

The House of Art, House of Bricks and the main building

THE ROGNER-BAD BLUMAU HOTEL | Blumau | Austria

Suddenly a sign looms – Rogner-Bad Blumau – and our relieved driver swings his carload of stressed passengers up a long winding drive toward the hotel. But we forget our irritation when we catch sight of the hotel. Located on the hillside is a surreal collection of buildings that would make even Dr Seuss look twice. Pink castles with golden onion-domed towers, oval eye-shaped structures with grass covered roofs, multicoloured textured walls, and in the centre, a steaming thermal mineral water lake.

Colourful and decorative, this hotel façade strikes a chord that wouldn't pass for architectural critique, but we are immediately amused and pleased by the contrast between this perky, exuberant building and its neatly manicured and ordered rural setting. It's visual fun. And as we were to find out, the hotel is also a place for serious relaxation and stress escape.

Designed by Friedensreich Hundertwasser, the famous Austrian artist and architect, the Rogner-Bad Blumau Spa Hotel is an unparalleled visual experience and drawcard for Austria's spa district of Styria. The grassed roofs and the total absence of any straight lines give the impression that many of the buildings are growing out of the ground. Hundertwasser believes that 'the straight line creates speed, speed creates stress'. Perhaps this philosophy inspired our taxi driver's roundabout route.

There has been plenty of architectural criticism of both Hundertwasser and his buildings. The hotel has been aptly described as a gingerbread fantasia, and it is certainly a modern take on the baroque castle. However, as a friend once said, aren't we lucky it's there so we can criticise it. Since the Rogner-Bad Blumau opened in 1998 it has enjoyed high levels of occupancy, and is popular for weekend breaks, so it demonstrably works as a hotel. Form hasn't triumphed over function here.

Once inside, relieved to have finally arrived, we are welcomed by smiling, sympathetic staff. Our room key is a bright blue wristwatch, a 'key-bracelet', with the inscription 'a life in harmony with nature'. Wear this and a wave of the wrist gains entry to all the guest facilities. Much more harmonious and easier to find than a plastic key card.

A LIFE IN HARMONY WITH NATURE

THE MORE DIFFERENT THINGS THERE ARE,
THE RICHER THE WORLD...

The outdoor pool

Eco friendly bedroom 1502

The mosaic tiled bathroom

Our room, high in the pink onion-topped tower, is spacious and quite plain. Its unvarnished wood and natural fabrics are certainly more sober than might be expected after the somewhat tipsy exterior. However, the sobriety is abandoned in the tiled mosaic patchwork of the bathroom. While it has the requisite fittings and an efficient shower, its cheerful, slightly crazy atmosphere is rarely found in bathroom design.

From our windows we can see the large outdoor thermal spa pool with its silver sprout water jets. And we imagine we can hear the sea, which is puzzling since we are in landlocked Austria. An inspection reveals a second, smaller pool adjacent to the main pool. Its wave-making machine is in full swing, sending crashing waves from one end of the pool to the other, to the delight of bathers enjoying the instant surf. We rise at daybreak to photograph the sunrise. Golden early morning sunlight filters through the low mist hanging over the hotel, and at the main entrance, a group of people is busy unloading a hot air balloon. In the distance, partly hidden by mist and trees, the gothic steeple of a nearby village church glints with the rising sun.

After choosing a healthy and hearty breakfast from the enormous variety on offer, we wander the tiled corridors connecting the therapy treatment rooms of the Holistic Health Institute. Guests traverse these corridors on their way to and from the various treatments, usually dressed in robes and slippers supplied by the hotel. This is a state of the art health spa as well as an architectural whimsy on a grand scale; delighting the eye and senses as it restores the spirit.

Many different stress-relieving treatments are available, from computer-controlled water-massage baths to advanced dietary treatments, but it was the music and sound therapy that intrigued us. Initially doubtful of its worth, we listened to the description of this therapy with raised eyebrows. The experience proved the better test. The therapy was developed by Wolfgang Koelbl, a holistic doctor, and it is unique to the Rogner-Bad Blumau. The recipient lies on a couch, which has an instrument like a xylophone underneath it. This is strummed, allowing both sound

Sound and music therapy

Hot air balloon with eye-shaped house and main building in background

and vibration to soothe the mind. Added to this are several layers of additional sounds, using instruments such as the monochord, Tibetan singing bowls, and brass gongs and a sound pyramid. Sound therapy was used in traditional Tibetan healing and by the Incas, and Dr Koelbl believes music is the path to the inner self. Cynical at first, we both rose from the couch feeling uplifted and relaxed, our heads ringing with the beautiful and unusual sounds.

The centrepiece of Rogner-Bad Blumau is the thermal pool with its restorative healing properties. Massaging water jets are strategically placed around the edges and at the centre of the pool, bliss for a travel weary body.

It is best to visit the pool at twilight, lying in the warm spa water and watching the sun go down before swimming through a short tunnel into the indoor pool. You can relax even further stretched out on a chaise then eat poolside or amble on to a leisurely dinner.

The two restaurants serve great food and wine which say more about good living than the spa environment – and there are no watchful calorie-counting attendants disguised as waiters to catch you out.

Go to this 'oasis of wellness' to relax, recuperate and be amused by the witty environment. During our stay, we didn't leave the hotel and its immediate surroundings, but there is masses to do besides just 'spa-ing out'. Activities include golf, ballooning and horseriding.

Restored and inspired, we boarded a hotel shuttle van headed for Vienna airport. Driving off, my last glance of the hotel through the rear window was to reassure myself that the three-day experience, staying in what may well be the world's first inhabitable work of art was not just imaginary.

Wall of the House of Art

How to get there: The Hotel
Rogner-Bad Blumau is located at
Blumau, 120 kilometres south of
Vienna, or 60 kilometres from Graz.
It can be reached by either train, taxi
or rental car.

For reservations:

Telephone: +43 3383 5100-0

Facsimile: +43 3383 5100-808

E-mail: resm@blum.rogner.co.at

Internet: www.rogner.com

43

MOONSTRUCK

HAND IN HAND, ON THE EDGE OF THE SAND,
THEY DANCED BY THE LIGHT OF THE MOON. Edward Lear

THE MOTU | Bora Bora | French Polynesia

Anchored just off-shore from the near-mythical South Pacific island of Bora Bora, is 'The Motu' – a special retreat on an island set apart. In Polynesian legend, Bora Bora is a sacred island, the first to rise out of the sea. Protected by a barrier reef and its blue crystalline lagoon, it is surrounded by a myriad of small motus – islets. It's from this that 'The Motu' takes its simple name.

The eternal lure of islands has drawn travellers in search of peace, quiet and isolation – or at least the illusion of it – to tropical arcadia such as this, from time immemorial. The soothing sound of waves lapping on the shore, or crashing on the distant reef, often lulls the stressed into a blissful state of relaxation and sleep. A stunning climate, spectacular scenery and beautiful beaches – for sunning on by day and strolls after-dinner in the moonlight – are on the 'wish list' of island-holiday seekers.

Searching for a place to stay in Bora Bora, we saw an artist's sketch of a new hotel in progress. Our inquiring fax drew this descriptive email response.

Dear Shelley-Maree, ia orana (hello)!

My name is Frédéric Lemoine-Romain, I'm the assistant of Denis de Schrevel (General Manager), we are both in charge of the two Sofitels of Bora Bora (Sofitel Coralia Marara & Sofitel Coralia Motu). As Denis is out of the island, I'm answering now to your fax. I can give you some of the following informations to help you :

- the Motu is a private and exclusive resort; with 20 deep overwater and 10 deluxe (built on the island) bungalows (total 30), around 60 persons max. living on this property

- the environnement of the Motu is really exceptionnal (natural coral gardens, small hill with tremendous and amazing vues (several all around), different plants, ambiance climate depending where you are on the island, facing the famous Otemanu mountain of Bora Bora (in the best angle vue), area of reproduction of the famous heron (protected or preserved area for us, this is also the logo of the Motu)...

The Motu – island in the sun

The frangipane flower

View from the Motu of Bora Bora's twin peaks

- for all those reasons we decided to developpe a specific concept to offer to our guests of the Motu :

1. Luxury and Sauvage

2. Simplicity and Authenticity

- Luxury: inside of each bungalow and in the communal area (materials used, furnitures...)

- Sauvage: outside of the bungalow considering the beauty of the nature (sea, lagoon, the island in itself, protection of the environnement, back to the nature for each guest, in a large majority coming from cities...)

- Simplicity: human size island (one hour walking round trip), where the communal area is the heart, for simplicity and comfort (welcome area, activities desk, lounge bar, restaurant in the same 'grand salon', panoramic one, closed from each bungalow...)

- Authenticity: in a real Tahitian ambiance (local staff from BOB), with local roofs, kohu wood used worked by Tahitian people knowing this wood very well, some of the employees able to give a real traditionnal and authentic touch for the guests that looked for it (barbecue on the island, explanations of tradition...)

- As it stays a small hotel, we can imagine offering to those exclusives guests something more than a hotel: like personnalization of all the different services guests of the Motu, for us, exclusives guests, will have a direct boat transfer from the airport to the Motu (if possible, check-in in the boat). This exclusif resort is not built to accept children and please no noise for our exclusives guests. Overwater and deluxe have the same space (49 m² inside + terasse), but overwater have add in each a round glass floor for the vue, and a large sundeck (12 m²) with outside shower + steps and ladder to go in the water. Deluxe bungalow, very deep overwater with sundeck open to the lagoon. 3 beaches, sunny, several spots to use in the nature for picnic, relaxing small local 'fare', outside barbecue... – As it is an upscale, private, and specific place, we added a permanent coordinator in charge of the stays of the guests, for a real personnalization and quality.

I really hope that this e-mail will help you to confirm to yourself, that we could probably be in your next edition, as soon as you will visiting us, you'll be, I'm sure!!!

Please receive our tropical and sincere best regards.

Frédéric Lemoine-Romain
Executive Assistant Manager

Overwater bungalow 121

Bathroom of 121

Boats at anchor in the lagoon

We started packing immediately. And here you can see for yourself much of what Frederic described so well. For those who seek a temporary escape, this is an ideal runaway destination. The high cost of living the South Seas' dream here is a price worth paying for something to remember long after you return to the real world.

SOMETIMES A MAN HITS UPON A PLACE TO WHICH HE
MYSTERIOUSLY FEELS THAT HE BELONGS W. Somerset Maugham

UNWIND...

SUN... SAND... DAYDREAM...

REFRESHED...

FLOWERS...SEABREEZES...

SLEEP... DREAM... RUNAWAY...

TROPICS...

PALM TREES...EDEN...

ESCAPE...   LAZE... SPELL... IDYLLIC ISLAND...

TIME...

...LOVE

The Motu at sunset

How to get there as fast as possible: fly to Papeete, then to Bora
Bora, and by boat to the Motu.

The Sofitel Coraha Motu	Telephone: + 689 67 70 46
Bora Bora	Facsimile: +689 67 74 03
FRENCH POLYNESIA	E-mail: h8989@accor-hotels.com

Goreme in distance, bathed in evening light

CAVING IN CAPPADOCIA

Millions of years ago volcanic eruptions and the forces of erosion sculpted a fanciful and extraordinary sandstone landscape in the remote valleys of Cappadocia, in central Turkey. Man has added to these outlandish and amazing natural forms over the centuries, carving houses, hermit cells, churches, catacombs and underground cities from the soft rock and pinnacles.

ESBELLI EVI HOUSE | Urgüp | Turkey

Esbelli Evi House at night

Driving down into the village of Urgüp, we're struck by the blending of landscape and buildings. Colour and shape merge to such a degree it is almost impossible to tell where the village begins and ends. From a distance, the houses appear to melt into the pale gold rock of the cliffs. Located at the edge of Urgüp and nestled against low cliffs is Esbelli Evi House, a restored cave pension. The bedrooms are probably the oldest in the hotel business, as they date back to the sixth century, while the upper building was added in the eighteenth century. The upper floor's reception and reading room are decorated with antique Turkish rugs and low brass tables, classic and elegant. Downstairs, the bedrooms are a labyrinth of caves hollowed out from the hillside's soft rock. The smooth honey-coloured stone of the walls is both cool and atmospheric. These cave rooms are simply furnished with kilim rugs, antique brass beds and some include a fireplace.

Bought and converted into a guesthouse a decade ago by owner Suha Ersov, Esbelli Evi House is easily the most interesting hotel in the area. Of the eight bedrooms, one was originally a kitchen, another a stable, and a third a wine pressing room. Suha prefers to run Esbelli Evi as a house rather than a hotel. He shows his guests the sitting-room, stocked with an eclectic range of books, CDs and chess sets, the kitchen with its well-stocked refrigerator, and a do-it-yourself laundry and tells them to make themselves at home.

Reception and reading room

Classic kilim rugs on the stone floors belonged to Suha's grandmother, and his mother made the traditional lace curtains, enhancing the feeling of being in a private home. Like home, there is no restaurant or room service, but the breakfast room on the rooftop patio serves tasty breads, hard-boiled eggs, fruit and coffee. Sitting in the morning sun drinking coffee and looking out over the village and mountains beyond seems a valid activity for quite some time. For lunch or dinner village restaurants just a stroll down the hill serve excellent local food and wine. A short drive from Esbelli House is the Gulludere and Kizilcukur Valleys, known as the Red and Rose Valleys. These are a fantasy of pink sandstone shapes and erosion-formed gullies that glow orange and red at sunset, attracting busloads of tourists in the busy season to watch from the vantagepoint of the car park. The valleys are a stunning sight, better viewed without a horde of onlookers, but worth seeing whenever.

Rock houses at Uchisar

The Kitchen Room cave bedroom once an old kitchen, the oven now the wardrobe.

In this spectacular landscape, hundreds of cone-shape rock forms have been gouged out over the centuries to serve as crude living accommodation, stables or churches. Doors and windows are often dozens of metres from the ground. On the valley's lower path, Ayvali Kilise (the Church of the Quince) is a cave church with wonderful interior wall paintings dating from the eleventh century. Scattered about this stone wonderland are occasional vineyards and orchards where a farmer or two may be seen toiling away behind a horse drawn plough. No television aerials or telephone poles intrude on a walk through this timeless landscape. Along the track we find a café carved in the rock, with log seats to enjoy Turkish coffee.

Some kilometres away, we drive through the village of Uchisar where colourful roadside market stalls lie at the foot of a cluster of towering rock houses typical of the area. Still further on, we stop to look over the village of Goreme. The vista is a dazzling array of rock formations, the architecture mixing recent conventional rock buildings with ancient conical houses and churches. All are aglow in the gold evening light. In the distance, the call to prayer breaks the deep silence, adding an eerie soundtrack to an already fantastical scene.

The following day we are to go hot-air ballooning, our first experience of this mode of flight. Owned, operated and piloted by husband and wife Lars-Eric More and Kaili Kidner, the Kapadokya Balloon Company flies two hot air balloons from April to November. This excursion means a very early morning wakeup call to first confirm that the weather is right. The day dawns stunning and perfect for flying with gas. On our arrival at 5.30 am, the balloons are inflated. Within minutes we are airborne ascending quietly into the warm early-morning light, standing in our cane basket lined with the local kilim carpet. As we climb, the sunrise etches long shadows into the amazing landscape. At two thousand feet I can appreciate the phrase 'putting all your eggs in one basket'. Feeling the breeze on your face as fresh air rather than a draught from aircraft air conditioning is far more pleasant, though you do feel a deal more fragile.

But we feel in capable hands, with our pilot in the same basket and happy to answer questions as she adjusts the burner above our head, and communicates with the other balloon and the ground crew. We descend to a few metres above the ground and pass so close to a group of apricot trees it is almost possible to reach out and pick the fruit before drifting lazily, dreamily up across the sky... Of course landing is a key issue of ballooning – what goes up must come down is a very apt saying, and there's no coming in for another try. The pilot has to get it right the first time. We are impressed by the perfect touchdown, the basket bypassing bumpy fields to drop neatly upright on the back of the Jeep's trailer. When I congratulate the pilot on the faultless landing, she admits it is the first time she has achieved a direct hit onto the trailer. Once down, the balloons are packed away by the ground crew while the passengers are treated to cherry juice, champagne and cake to celebrate the flight. 'Ballooning is one of the most beautiful things you can do in your life,' Suha had told us. We agree – flying over the stunning lunar-like landscape of Cappadocia on such a magnificent morning has added to an unforgettable experience.

Room 16, cave bedroom with fire place.

Balloon over Goreme.

OUR LAST MOMENTS IN TURKEY WERE HAPPY ONES,

AS WE DISCOVERED ISTANBUL AIRPORT HAS A MASSIVE
FREE TASTING COUNTER OF TURKISH DELIGHT, IN EVERY FLAVOUR

How to get there: We flew from Istanbul* to Kayseri on Turkish
Airlines (1 hour 30 minutes) Either hire a car at the airport or arrange
through Turkish Airlines for a shuttle bus transfer directly from Kayseri
to Urgüp, delivered to the door of Esbelli Evi House.

Esbelli Evi House	Telephone: +90 384 341 3395
Urgüp	Facsimile: +90 384 341 8848
Cappadocia	E-mail: suha@esbelli.com.tr
TURKEY	Internet: www.esbelli.com.tr

Kapadokya Balloons, Goreme.

Lars-Eric More and Kaili Kidner

E-mail: fly@kapadokyaballons.com

Goreme, Cappadocia, Turkey

EAU DE COLOGNE

You certainly can't miss this hotel, the tallest building by far in the neighbourhood. The former water reservoir, once Europe's largest, has been transformed into a contemporary and intriguing hotel.

The water tower was built between 1868 and 1872 by an English engineer, but it was made obsolete by an underground watermain system laid in the early 1900s. During World War II the lower floors of the water tower served as an air-raid shelter, but the upper floors were partially destroyed.

In the 1980s, plans were conceived to convert the neglected building into a hotel. After four years of reconstruction work, including the rebuilding of the top floors and inserting windows in the blind arches, the Hotel in Watertower opened to guests in 1990.

The architectural monument is a bricklayer's heaven, with old and new brickwork a major feature of the interior, particularly in the reception. Eleven-metre-high brick pillars with steel connecting bridges suspended across the core of the tower accentuate the interior's feeling of height and optical illusion. Furnishings were chosen by French designer Andrée Putman, an appropriate choice for this ultimate recycling project since she has expressed a belief in design being redemptive and a goal of creating things that last.

For the tower's new vocation as a hotel, she has used a cylindrical theme for many of the furnishings – armchairs, wall lamps, occasional tables, carpets and door handles appear as whole or halved cylinders.

Counter-pointing the rich brown of the bricks are dark wenge wood, and a palette of vanilla and sand tones, with rich yellow and royal blue used on velvet-covered furniture reminiscent of Art Deco.

The reception desks in the hotel lobby are an amusing play on the round theme, with the two halves forming a mirror image, an unusual effect for the arriving and departing guest. Time whiled away in the bar, also semi-circular, can induce confusion as you amble back to your room, when one side of the hotel is the same as the other. In this case, seeing double is not always a result of drinking too much. But even the strictly sober may not want to look down as they walk across metal bridging to their rooms.

The view from the roof-top terrace circling the restaurant is spectacular, taking in the medieval and modern city of Cologne, its trademark twin-towered cathedral, and the river Rhine. The restaurant interior seems somewhat at odds with the rest of the hotel design, but the food is excellent and the vista no less so. On a clear day this is an ideal vantagepoint for a visual tour of the city.

The Wasserturm's location makes for quiet surroundings more typical of a country hotel than one close to the centre of a major European city. It is a handy refuge for anyone exhibiting or visiting the myriad of trade fairs hosted by Cologne, which range from fashion to photography to food.

If you prefer to stay sequestered in the tower, choose one of the studio rooms, which feel more like apartments. Whitewashed and spacious, they have great curved windows, screened to soften and diffuse the light.

The other imposing structure on the skyline is the Gothic Cathedral, which was begun in 1248 and completed in 1880. It attracts visitors and pilgrims to see its golden shrine of the Magi. The cathedral's distinctive spires are an enduring symbol of a city with many Romanesque churches. Other attractions are shopping in the Old Town, sailing on the Rhine River or visiting museums. The great variety of museums include one with Europe's largest collection of American Pop art, a Beatles museum and the taste-sensational Museum of Chocolate.

Curved lines in the bathroom

Living room of studio bedroom

At the Imhoff-Stollwerck-Museum – which is itself an interesting building on a peninsular jutting out into the Rhine – there is the opportunity to explore the history and culture of chocolate. 'Light is shed on the dark past of this brown delicacy!' With a tropical hot house that is full of cocoa trees and exotic plants; a working chocolate factory where visitors can see how chocolate bars, truffles and hollow Easter bunnies are made, and a fountain that is actually flowing with hot chocolate, this museum is a real must to visit, smell and taste. And yes, there is a museum shop as well, in addition to a river terrace restaurant to rest up at if all that cacao has gone to your head!

The bronze Wasserturm room key, a miniature version of the Watertower, is far too heavy to forget to leave at reception.

The room key, hotel in miniature

Hotel im Wasserturm Kaygasse 2 – 50676 Koln GERMANY	Telephone: +49 2 21 – 200 80
	Facsimile: +49 2 21 – 2 00 88 88
The Chocolate Museum: www.koeln.org/imhoff-stollwerck-museum/english	

The Clarence Hotel and the Grattan Bridge over the River Liffey

BOOMTOWN

SUPPOSE OUR ROOMS AT THE HOTEL WERE BESIDE EACH OTHER
AND ANY FOOLING WENT ON... James Joyce, from Ulysses

These words, forming a pink lettered neon sign, were written across the top of the
Clarence Hotel when I first visited Dublin in October of 1997. It was a temporary
installation, part of the Dublin Literary Festival. Neon quotes appeared all over the
city centre, recalling the words of writers who have lived in and written about
Dublin – Joyce, Shaw, Beckett, Swift, Wilde... I wish these modern, poetic sign
writings had been retained, as a unique tribute to the writers who shaped the literary
heritage of this vital city. Jonathan Swift, the eighteenth-century author of *Gulliver's
Travels*, would not recognise the new dynamic Dublin, which he once described as
'the most disagreeable place in Europe'. W B Yeats referred to his home town as
'blind and ignorant'. Criticised roundly by most of the writers now lionised by
the city they spurned, contemporary Dublin is a favoured European weekend
destination, the most visited city after Paris.

THE CLARENCE HOTEL | Dublin | Ireland

Like the French capital, it is a city for walking – to savour the architecture and rub shoulders with Dubliners. With a fine collection of low-rise eighteenth-century buildings, wide streets and intimate pubs, this is a city of human proportions. Molly Malone may be a fond memory, but street traders and buskers still work the busy streets. The heart of a revitalised Eire, modern Dublin has more buzz than blarney. The Ireland of leprechauns and begorrahs, for so long part of the Irish myth, is not to be found here, although the brogue is still evident. The Clarence Hotel edges a maze of cobbled streets known as the Temple Bar district, the city's social hub. The building's solid stone frontage overlooks the River Liffey, situated on Dublin's 'left bank', between the Grattan and Ha'penny Bridges.

From its beginnings as a railway hotel in 1852, the Clarence has projected architectural dignity, a quality it retained even at its most shabby in the 1970s. Generations of Guinness and whiskey drinkers have frequented its bars. Bought by Bono and The Edge, members of the Dublin-based rock group U2, the Clarence has been restored as a spacious and aristocratic feeling small hotel. A pale background of oak, leather and stone sets off its arts and craft style. Traditional and contemporary are cleverly combined, with a simplicity reminiscent of Shaker design. Hotel staff are dressed in sharp grey suits with just a hint of the cassock in the cut of their jackets.

The warm relaxing environment is underpinned by the use of rich colour – crimson, royal blue, purple, gold and chocolate – never all combined in the one scheme. Colourful and covetable original artwork by Irish artist Guggi is on show throughout the hotel.

The Study projects the feel of a country house or a gentlemen's club. This is a comfortable place to settle into the leather chairs, read the newspapers and sip coffee or something stronger as the soft Irish light filters through the high windows.

The stylish Octagon bar and especially the snug wood-panelled back bar tempt you to an Irish beer or whiskey, in that quintessential Irish establishment, the pub.

In the former ballroom, the Tea Room Restaurant offers a mouth-watering menu. Posted on the wall of the 'back door' to the Clarence, in Temple Bar, this also attracts passers-by in search of good food.

The Reading Room Study

The penthouse suite with grand piano, bar, great sound system, private garden terrace and open air hot tub is a place to feel like a visiting member of the rock aristocracy. It offers one of the best views of Dublin, across to the Wicklow mountains and Dublin Bay.

If you want to get out and about, it is a short stroll to Grafton Street shopping, galleries, theatres, cafés, restaurants, clubs and bars, both traditional and contemporary. An impressive collection of contemporary design is on display and for sale in the Irish Craft Centre, five minutes' walk from the hotel. The parks of Merrion Square and St Stephen's Green are the city's 'emerald islands'. They are lovely even on 'soft days', an Irish euphemism for rainy weather.

A bedroom view

The 'Celtic Tiger' can be heard as well as seen, with renovation and rebuilding underway throughout the city and new hotels, restaurants and bars opening at a rapid rate in response to the growing number of visitors and locals. Ireland's economic success is founded on benevolent tax laws for overseas investors and European Union money. The mood of confidence and the country's positive international profile have seen many ex-pats return to their homeland to share in its new found pride.

When the sun goes down, this is a party town. Not much of the old Irish puritanism is here – Dublin has the youngest population in Ireland, and even the no longer young act it. The city stays up late. The huge number of pubs caters for virtually every musical taste from folk through to contemporary. Many weekend 'riverdancers' who come to trip the light fantastic go home with a hangover they may not think so grand on Monday.

Visitors can retrace the steps of past Dublin writers on the Literary Pub Crawl, the best excuse for drinking and talking I've ever heard. Actors, not short of a well-crafted witty line themselves, guide the tours of pubs where many of the city's famous (and infamous) drank and claimed their inspiration. Soaking up 'culture' while testing the local beverages is an appealing combination even now.

For somewhere much quieter, no talking or drinking allowed, the Library at Trinity College is a bibliophile's dream, with its timber-vaulted ceiling and rows of books. The university is also the guardian of the Book of Kells, the treasured ninth century illuminated manuscript of the Gospels.

Dublin was the focal point of the struggle for and against home rule. The General Post Office still bears the scars of the violent 1916 Easter Uprising, and it remains the favourite starting point for demonstrations. Also the site of the 1921 Declaration of Independence, the post office is on O'Connell Street, a broad avenue on the north side of the River Liffey, now seen as the less gentrified 'new' city.

Lift detail

The Penthouse hot tub

The Clarence Hotel	Telephone: +353 1 670 9000
6 – 8 Wellington Quay	
Dublin 2	Facsimile: +353 1 670 7800
IRELAND	
For information on Dublin visit www.ireland.com/dublin/essentials	

The Ice Hotel at night, with the Aurora Borealis

IN THE HALL OF THE MOUNTAIN KING

Some twenty miles inside the Arctic Circle, the temperature twenty-five degrees below freezing, Lapland is no place for fashion victims. Here you wear the clothes the hotel has determined are right for the conditions – at least the outer garments. When you feel just how cold it is here, you'll be happy to climb into the Michelin-man insulation suits and the fur hats provided.

THE ICE HOTEL | Jukkasjärvi | Sweden

The Ice Hotel is in Swedish Lapland, in the small village of Jukkasjarvi, in the heart of reindeer-herding territory. It takes two hours or so to fly from Stockholm to the airport of Kiruna. There you choose to be met by the hotel shuttle bus for the ten-minute ride to Jukkasjarvi or a husky drawn sled for a two hour transfer with a difference.

Rooms can be reserved only from November through to May – and even then only if it is cold enough. For this is a hotel that re-invents itself every year according to the weather. It depends on ice for both its form and its fame. Winter's onset dictates the building of the Ice Hotel while the arrival of spring heralds its self-destruction. The temperature warms up; the hotel melts down. The ultimate spring clean.

The biggest igloo in the world, the Ice Hotel is literally sculpted from nearby river ice. Building begins at the end of October, or during November, depending on weather conditions. It takes temperatures of three degrees below freezing, and some six to eight weeks work to construct the shell. Snow cannons spray thirty thousand tonnes of manufactured snow onto specially made metal moulds. Once the snow is sufficiently hard the moulds are removed. As the exterior construction proceeds, the interior structure and decoration begins. Bearing walls and pillars, furniture and

The entrance hall

A bedroom, chill factor minus five

sculptures are made from huge cylindrical iceblocks cut out from the frozen river with a special ice saw. By mid January, cold permitting, the building is completed.

The result is a hotel that can accommodate 100 people, and which includes a bar, cinema and chapel. The stunning entrance hall is an arched cavern with a snow ceiling and windows of translucent iceblocks. Because the river is slow running, the ice freezes with few air bubbles and the density gives it a distinct blue glow. This colonnade of ice is complete with a grand chandelier, made entirely of ice, and lit with optical fibres.

Every year the hotel takes on a different design. The annual rebuilding gives the hotel designers opportunity to refine their ideas, and increase their 'snow-how'. Local ice sculptors add their work to the interior, carving out a variety of whimsical pieces, from bears and huskies to ice televisions and fans.

Entering the grand reception hall is to arrive in another realm, an ice palace where a glittering crystal power rules supreme. The King of Cold's stern domain is white, sparkling clear, and majestically lit with a mass of candles. The omnipresent silence inside that pervades this cool chamber invites whispers rather than normal speech.

And yet it seems warm inside, even though it is only minus five degrees approximately. After the fiercely chilling outside air it feels positively warm.

Having greeted us warmly at the frozen reception desk, our igloo guide Thor points out that few guests lounge about in the lobby to people watch. That's not surprising – the seats are actually ice blocks covered with reindeer skins.

All the furniture in the hotel is made of ice – and that includes the beds, also blanketed with reindeer skins. The choice of rooms ranges from standard through to suites, usually more richly decorated. Rooms are made individual by artworks and sculptures, although ice is common to all. White linen curtains serve for bedroom doors. There are no heaters or hairdryers, or even bathrooms – these are located in another building.

On the night we stayed, the in-house movie theatre (with ice bench seats, upholstered in fur) screened the latest Batman movie with Arnold Schwarzenegger as the evil Iceman. In this climate the audience related more to the villain than the hero.

The Ice Hotel during the day

Road sign

The hotel bar is open to guests and visitors. But lean too long on this bar and you'll be a permanent fixture. The Absolut Vodka company is a partner in the Ice Hotel, and its brand is inevitably the only vodka available. The other product placement is at the bar entrance; the opening is cut in the distinctive shape of the Absolut Vodka bottle. Beer is off the menu, as its low alcohol content means it would freeze in the cool atmosphere.

A post-nuptial party was held in the bar after a wedding celebrated in the beautiful ice chapel, where the seats as well as the bride were clad in fur. The wedding photographs gave the phrase 'freeze-frame' a new meaning. The newlyweds spent the first night of their honeymoon in the ice bridal suite. There are double sleeping bags.

On that same night guests were treated to an amazing bonus – the eerily beautiful spectacle of the Aurora Borealis. This luminous atmospheric phenomenon is triggered when particles from the sun collide with the earth's magnetic field. Here it is called the Northern Lights, and streaks of yellow, green, crimson and rose are painted across the starry Arctic sky as if some celestial artist is at work.

When it is time to chill out, guests are zipped into specially made Arctic survival sleeping bags designed to withstand temperatures down to minus 25 to minus 30 degrees. The warm under-layers you are sensibly wearing are kept on, and your outer-clothes stay snug in the sleeping bag with you. During the pre-retirement briefing, the guide advises sleeping on your back to avoid the possibility of your face freezing to the sleeping bag.

Certificate of Coldworthiness

Lying in an all white ice bedroom, surrounded by a total and deep quiet, flickering shadows thrown by the flickering candlelight, is like being inside a snow cave deep within a mountain. The room temperature varies between minus four to minus nine degrees Centigrade, depending on how cold it is outside and the number of overnight guests – and you pay for this experience! Surprisingly, many say they slept soundly and warmly throughout the night.

In the morning you are woken with room service bearing hot berry juice. A traditional sauna lures, authenticated by the Swedish Sauna Academy, whose motto is 'in sauna veritas' – in the sauna, truth is revealed. Now you are conditioned to the chill factor, the steamy heat can come as a bit of a shock.

With a reconditioned thermostat, you can deal to a generous Scandinavian breakfast in the restaurant across the road. The cold air heightens the appetite for cuisine from the Lapland larder: game, berries, local venison and fish such as Arctic char.

The overnight experience can be extended with a stay in nearby wooden chalets, with full-on central heating. Daytime activities include safaris, with a team of ten to twelve huskies leading each expedition. There are more dogs than people in Jukkasjärvi. More than 900 sled dogs – Siberian and Alaskan huskies – are ready to take you on a fast trip through the Laplandic landscape of frozen lakes and snow-dressed pine forests.

Impatient to be off, the dogs bark furiously while waiting. Once they start pulling their load, they are contentedly quiet, and all that can be heard is their padding feet and the sound of the sled gliding across the snow.

Parking outside the Ice Hotel is for snowbikes rather than the usual cars. The bikes cover the icy ground more efficiently than any car, although the chill factor is vastly greater. Kicksleds are another mode of transport seen in the parking lot. This is a sort of wooden chair on metal runners, propelled like a scooter. Driving lessons quickly qualify drivers for both snowbikes and kicksleds, which can be used for short trips or longer expeditions to wilderness camps.

Husky team transfer sled to the airport

Now in its ninth year, the Ice Hotel has been a successful venture. Last year, nearly four thousand guests stayed overnight, while twenty thousand day visitors saw the massive snow and ice sculpture and enjoyed the adventure activities on offer in this stunning spot on top of the world.

Adventurers staying over in the Ice Hotel are presented with a certificate on their departure, as a permanent reminder of their igloo experience. They may have been comforted to know that the Cold Center, specialists in sub-zero physiology, was close at hand, in nearby Kiruna.

Jukkas AB	Telephone: +46 980 66800
The Ice Hotel	
Marknadsvagen 63	Facsimile: +46 980 66890
S-981 91 Jukkasjärvi	Email: reception@jukkas.se
SWEDEN	Internet: www.jukkas.se

URBAN RETREAT

The Tawaraya turns away from the street to face inward to privacy, peace and serenity. In a modern city with its share of urban chaos, tranquillity rules in this ryokan. Nearly three hundred years old, the traditional Japanese inn is dignified but not paralysed by the past.

The attributes of modern living are here but gracefully hidden, carefully shrouded in beautiful textiles or placed in containers that hide their form. You, honoured guest, also have your special place in this ordered environment. Other than a small and beautiful library that I'd like transplanted to my own home, there are no public spaces where you might confront other guests. Often, you encounter no one – even the staff seem to materialise rather than exist. Only room-service food is available, but what food to stay in for. And there is the exquisite fussing of the staff, serenely mannered but ever alert to your smallest needs.

The exterior of the Tawaraya

The Reception

In a plain narrow street in central Kyoto you can take refuge behind the Tawaraya's walls, embrace solitude or enjoy companionship, contemplate, rest, be restored.

A pervading air of calm provides a sanctuary from the relentless race of contemporary life. Here are the real luxuries of silence, space and gourmet food – asceticism without sacrifice. Traditional Japanese architecture and innkeeping combine, providing a marvellous experience that is relevant and viable. Refined, luxurious, it is essentially a simple way of life, ordered and arranged.

Within these walls, the guest is the focus. You must submit to the routine and rhythms that are the ritual of staying in a ryokan. This is not an experience for those of harried temperament. Be prepared to adjust to the formality, the service and manners that are unlike any other style of hotel. Your role is that of honoured guest.

Having left your shoes and donned slippers at the entrance, you shed your travel clothes, and choose from the wardrobe of special kimonos and yukatas in your room. Slide back the shoji screens to contemplate the serene private gardens – with a stone pool where water flows from a bamboo tap into the stone basin below, leafy maple trees and moss covered stone lanterns.

Rooms are simple, gracefully decorated with traditional furniture, and some Western pieces for those who find it hard to sit on the floor. Traditional tatami matting is laid on the floor, sumptuous brocades cover the telephone and other reminders of the real world.

Your room is dual purpose, by day a living and dining room, at night transformed into a bedroom when a futon is made up for you.

The bathroom is an essay in contrast – you can soak and relax in a traditional Japanese bath, a deep cedar tub kept constantly full of hot water by apparently invisible attendants, or marvel at the high-tech toilet with its array of flashing lights and symbols, appropriately hidden from view.

The evening banquet looked too beautiful to eat. Visually stunning compositions are served by our smiling kimono clad lady-in-waiting who appears on soundless slippered feet, as if from out of the walls rather than through sliding doors.

Presented on delicate Japanese pottery, each dish tastes exquisite. I start writing down a description of the courses in order to remember them but several sakes later both my handwriting and descriptive abilities become blurred. I can no longer focus even with what must be the world's most beautiful hotel stationery and pens at my disposal.

Our ten-course dinner is cooked, arranged and served with absolute artistry. It culminates with a simple grapefruit jelly served in a grapefruit shell framed by its porcelain dish – a dessert that deserves to be enshrined.

This is followed by a deepest sleep in the softest futon after which you are woken with morning newspapers and pots of tea.

Beautiful objects and changing table scenes in the corridors of the hotel reflect the seasons and events: May 5, horse racing; April, cherry blossom time; November, autumn leaves...

Room service

The Gyosuan (morning light) Room

The bathroom

Authenticity, or at least the illusion of authenticity, combines with luxury and service to harness past and present into a harmonious parallel.

Here you are surrounded by people who ease out the little inconveniences that make or mar the quality of life. They minister to the needs of guests with ceremony and elegance: service is an artform. Your lasting memories will be of the faultless manners that characterise this other-world Kyoto. That alone is worth the considerable expense. To be treated with such distinction, no matter who you are, invites mirror behaviour. A taste of old-world courtesy and the opportunity to practise it yourself is another gain.

The Satow family has owned the Tawaraya Inn for eleven generations and it is now run with gentle precision, by Mrs Toshi Okazaki Satow.

If you must venture out...

Kyoto is the ancient imperial capital, and it is here that the classic image of Japan survives. Behind the walls of the renowned temples, shrines, imperial villas and gardens is the traditional calm of Japanese culture. It hides behind the frenetic urban sprawl, with its traffic, neon signs, shopping arcades, crowded streets and pachinko parlours. The geisha quarter of Gion was the setting for Arthur Golden's book *Memoirs of A Geisha*.

The Fuji Room from the garden – looking in at peace.

In the busy streets, swirling masses of young Japanese girls chatter and laugh into their tiny pastel cellphones.

The Ten-you restaurant, a branch of the Tawaraya is only two minutes walk for a tempura lunch or dinner, or there is the famous Kawamichiya noodle shop.

You will return to your refuge with a sense of relief, ready for its seductive shot of calmness and tranquillity in an otherwise frantic life. The ryokan's enclosed world is perfect for restoring balance after an excursion into this hectic city. A willing capitulation to the order of the ryokan encourages you to slow down, and surrender the tension you arrived with.

Departure is a ceremony in itself. The staff farewell sees the taxi out of sight, vesting the departure with such dignity you determine to return, to be treated again as the honoured guest.

How to get there: We flew into Kansai, one of the most orderly and attractive airports in the world, took the train directly from there to Kyoto, an hour's journey, and then a taxi to the Tawaraya. Alternatively, travel by bullet train from Tokyo.

The Tawaraya Inn Fuyacho, Oike- Sagaru Nakagyo-Ku, Kyoto 604 – 8094 JAPAN	Telephone: + 81 75 211 5566
	Facsimile: + 81 75 211 2204

The Mosaic, entrance to the gardens of the Villa d'Este

THE VILLA D'ESTE | Lake Como | Italy

DOLCE VITA

One of the quintessential grand hotels of Europe, set in magnificent Renaissance gardens on the edge of Lake Como, the Villa d'Este has a romantic history worthy of an opera.

The gardens, planted when the estate was created in 1568, are wonderfully established. In the ten-acre private park of the Villa d'Este, carpets of lawns are punctuated with Italian cypresses, magnolias, horse chestnuts and well-placed statues. The magnificent centrepiece is the eighteenth-century mosaic, classed as an Italian national treasure. Its appealing symmetry screens an outdoor room with a central fish pond. Beyond, two rows of cypress trees lead up the hill past a cascade of fountains to the Grotto of Hercules. Behind it, thick woodlands overlook the deep waters of Lake Como.

From here it is a short climb to the fortifications, a collection of battlements and towers built by a woman to amuse a man. Soon after the death of her elderly husband, the Marquis Calderara, the ballerina La Pelusina, then the owner of the Villa d'Este, remarried a young Napeolonic general. Worried that he might feel nostalgic for warring, she gave him his own fort to keep him at home, and he happily played soldiers here. Now it gives guests somewhere to walk to and exercise off the splendid food.

The Villa d'Este is a legendary hotel, and has been described as 'not a hotel where you just stay, it's a hotel where you settle'. It draws its guests from the upper reaches of the old and new European and American society. Lake Como lured Greeks and Romans, Celts and Renaissance Europeans years before Americans and the Hollywood 'aristocracy' discovered it. Cardinals and princesses have also lived here and it has been a welcome refuge for royalty and for revolutionaries. The Princess of Wales – Princess Caroline of Brunswick, the unhappy wife of King George IV – lived here for five years from 1815 to 1820, and the Empress Maria Fedorowna, wife of the Russian Tsar, rented the villa for two weeks in 1868 and then ended up staying for two years.

The lobby

The classic façade of the Queen's Building at the Villa d'Este, built in 1856, named after Princess Caroline, wife of George IV . Terracotta, with trompe l'oeil shutters and trim, the annex's deep red façade is decorated with emblems of the Italian provinces.

The main building of the Villa d'Este is a white neoclassica palazzo, from the sixteenth century, designed by the architect Pellegrino Pellegrini. Enter through a narrow revolving door and you arrive in the sixteenth-century lobby, a blue and gold salon with marble floors, vaulted ceilings and Murano glass chandeliers. There is a gentle grandeur throughout, the furniture is usually Empire, upholstered in silk and velvet, and antique accessories are everywhere. However, this is not a museum, in either its furnishings or mood.

Here still is the grand European-style service, but without the old pomp and circumstance: you are made welcome, and the hotel feels gracious and serene, with an opulence that is natural, not fake, and comfortable, not formal. Take the double marble staircase or the elevator lined in Como silk brocade to your gracious and generously proportioned room. The shutters are opened on your arrival, so you may admire the stunning view from the balcony, one said to have inspired the invention of photography. This is a lake of legendary allure, its majestic beauty an attraction to visitors since Roman times. Ringed by mountains, its placid waters are constantly ruffled by sailing boats, water taxis, ferries and water-skiers. Lake Como is circled with the grand villas of the aristocracy and the newly rich and famous. Little villages in ice-cream colours sit at its green edges, and all are best seen from the water.

Here you can be pampered and calmed, only thirty minutes from the bustle of Milan, in this place for lovers – of gardens, and of elegance, and of each other.

You can take the Villa's private launch or hire one of the sleek wooden motorboats to visit the beautiful villages of Bellagio and Varenna, or you can be perfectly content to sit on the terrace and enjoy the view. While it is romantic, it is not merely chocolate box pretty. The tranquillity is tempered with the drama of mountains, and the light changes constantly.

Suite Room

The Veranda restaurant salon opens on each side to the sculpted gardens and, at the front, to the lake – where best to sit is the first decision. Next is the choice of divine food with painterly presentation and heavenly flavours. Here you may eat the food and then buy the Villa d'Este's deluxe recipe book, or attend cookery classes presided over by the master chef. Visiting to take lunch, or dinner, would be a reasonable compromise if you were not able to stay here. After lunch, wander the manicured gardens and paths, walk under the arcades covered with jasmine and wisteria, watch the lake from the terrace with its plane trees; one, in the middle of the terrace, is more than six hundred years old. For the more energetic, there is a health club discreetly placed in the grounds. A heated swimming pool floats lazily on the lake, its teak decks moving with the swell like a boat.

The Canova Room

Villa d'Este has a long pedigree and a celebrated guest list. The words 'grand hotel' evoke another era, more gracious and less hurried than our own. Keeping up with the times can be difficult, however, and not every grand hotel is as grand as it once was. Much stays the same at the Villa d'Este but it has moved itself from being an old to a new grand hotel, proving that things that were great can continue to be so. Consistently voted one of the world's top hotels, it gives considerable value for the considerable money it costs to stay here. This is a place to spoil yourself, an ultimate and memorable extravagance, and a delicious slice of la dolce vita.

The teak-decked swimming pool floats on the lake

The Villa d'Este Grand Hotel and Sporting Club	Telephone: +39 31 3481
22012 Cernobbio	Facsimile: +39 31 348844
Lago Como	E-mail: info@villadeste.it
ITALY	Internet: www.villadeste.it
Open from March to November	

CIRCUS CIRCUS

Roll up, roll up, to the Biggest Show on Earth… an astounding 30.5 million people visit Las Vegas every year to see the constant spectacle of this town built on chance. The performance is the clash of the Titans come true, a showdown amongst mega-hotels competing for attention.

A glittering mecca for tourists, Las Vegas is now more of an entertainment than a gambling destination. Although you can gamble even at the airport, people come here more for the performance than for the casinos, which are now common in most American cities. For Las Vegas casino-resort owners, this means expanding what they offer to attract and keep customers within the walls of their hotels once they get there.

Is it a hotel or a city? The size of the Luxor Hotel is such that guests need maps. Ours covered just one side of this black glass pyramid with its 4,476 rooms. Las Vegas claims to have nineteen of the world's twenty biggest hotels. The Bellagio, with 3,025 rooms is small by the city's standards – the MGM Grand has 5,005. In total there are around 120,000 rooms for rent.

The glass pyramid of the Luxor hotel, with Sphinx

Inside the Luxor; reception to the left – with an appropriately named shop for kids: Tiny Tuts

Las Vegas is America's fastest growing city. Some six thousand people move here every month – these include aspiring performers in search of employment in the ever-multiplying hotel casinos, or families and retirees looking for a place in the sun. Every one of them are attracted by the benign weather, bright lights, low taxes and affordable housing.

By day, the urban landscape is a strangely dull one. But come sundown, it is etched in neon and lights, and then it's show-time! Day and night, Las Vegas has a streetscape made up almost entirely of other cities' skylines: New York, Gaza's Pyramid (just one), Paris with the Eiffel Tower, Venice with canals and gondolas, Bellagio with Lake Como.

America's images and icons increasingly colonise the world, now it seems that it is taking something of other countries back – souvenirs on a grand scale. Is a Museum of the World being created here, a world in miniature, where Americans, at least, don't need passports and travellers' cheques? Here is Pocket Paris, Pocket New York and Pocket Venice, in scale and most of the key sights conveniently packaged close together for a concentrated and convenient visit. The city is a cheerful pastiche, with copies and caricatures of famous landmarks from around the world, sanitised and re-sized.

Conspicuous consumption is everywhere, from the bargain all-you-can-eat buffets to energy gobbling night-light extravaganzas. To some it is a display of conspicuous waste, one example being the destruction of old hotels to build new ones. You can see a video of the 'implosion' of the old Aladdin Hotel on the website of the new Aladdin.

New York, New York; the tallest hotel of course, re-creates most of that city's famous landmarks, the Manhattan skyline with the Empire State and Chrysler Buildings, Brooklyn Bridge, Times Square and the Statue of Liberty. Central Park is the casino's setting. The Manhattan Express is the world's first 'heartline' twist and dive roller coaster.

Treasure Island, home of the mock sea battle between two galleons, one crewed by British imperialists, the other by American buccaneers. The British captain goes down with his ship – and both pop up a few minutes later, ready for the next performance.

It's hard to see everything clamouring for your attention here. The tackiness is almost endearing in this show-off town which, like a kid, is out to impress – look at me, no me, HEY, ME!

Vegas caters both to the masses and to the elite; with a diverse range of entertainment, from pirate-themed Treasure Island, magicians and tiger tamers Siegfried and Roy to artists such as Van Gogh and Monet, 'now appearing' at the Bellagio Art Gallery. Shopping, wedding chapels, the Liberace Museum, and a museum for old neon signs also draw the crowds. When visitor numbers peak at weekends, so too do hotel room prices.

The Bellagio and its fountains that dance to music

This is the experience economy at its zenith, where the artificial is accepted as natural: dancing fountains, erupting volcanos, the captain going down with his ship every hour on the hour after dusk; and Atlantis destroyed hourly in a nine-minute apocalypse. Open 24/7, this is Vegas Mean Time, where sunrise and sunset occur at sixty-minute intervals in Caesar's Palace at the Forum.

You can boldly go where no man has gone before, at the Star Trek enterprise in the Las Vegas Hilton. This was the best casino styling, in keeping with the space theme. The warp speed concept seems very appropriate to Vegas, home of virtual reality. Or explore the Pharaoh's tomb, without the heat and flies, at the Luxor.

Geographically themed hotels continue to open. Paris Vegas is to have a fifty-storey tall, half-size replica of the Eiffel Tower, complete with restaurant part way up and a top floor viewing platform. Other faux French landmarks include the Paris Opéra, the Louvre, the Arc de Triomphe and the Hôtel de Ville. Inside the casino a replica of the Pont Alexander III bridge will overlook shops and lead to the Eiffel Tower elevators. Eight French-inspired restaurants will include Le Pool Café; and Le Village Buffet. Le Casino will be trés grand of course, with cobblestone paths and a forty-foot ceiling mural painted to look like the Parisian sky.

The Excalibur, home to the RoundTable Buffet,
Sir Galahad's RibRoom, Lance-a-Lotta Pasta
Restaurant and King Arthur's Tournament.

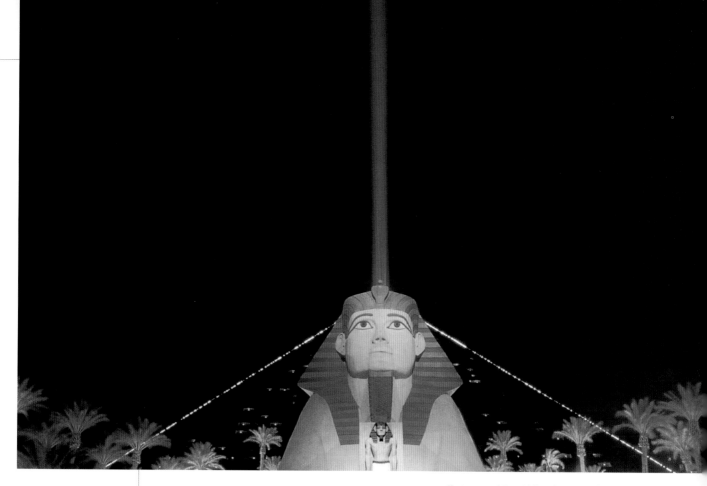

The Luxor at night, with laser beam to guide you home.

Costing US$1.6 billion, The Bellagio is the most expensive hotel ever built. It features a $300 million art collection, and branches of Tiffany, Armani and Prada. One of the few hotels that look good during the daylight hours, it is themed on Italy's Lake Como and the shore-side town of Bellagio. Italianate buildings with balustraded terraces surround a quarter-mile long artificial lake, to create an authentic atmosphere, except for the 36-storey hotel looming up behind and its syncopated fountains leaping high into the air. The Venetian, with its Piazza San Marco, a 315-foot high reproduction of the Campanile and arched bridges, has gondoliers to row you on the canal winding through the shopping mall.

In a town where spectacle is everything, and more of it arriving by the minute, the old Peggy Lee song 'Is that all there is?' comes to mind. With such sensory overload, it may well be true that excitement can become boring through repetition. Here high-rolling resort hotels are bidding to outperform their rivals. Vegas hoteliers must be showmen and ringmasters in this Entertainment Capital of the World, where all the hotels are in show business.

Vegas on the Internet:

www.visitlasvegas.com

www.vegaslounge.com

www.vegas.com

www.lasvegaslife.com

'LONDON; A NATION, NOT A CITY...' Benjamin Disraeli

LONDON PRIDE

A little perennial plant, London Pride is symbolic of the enduring spirit of London, a city that survived the Great Fire of 1666, and the bombing Blitz of World War II. One of the great cultural melting-pot cities of the world, London absorbs and transforms those who arrive from other countries. Now home to almost every race and religion, this vast city attracts a constant wave of visitors.

Britain's pomp and pageantry, really a formalised show business that is associated with an aristocracy headed by the Royals, continues to be one of London's major tourist attractions. Ceremonies like the Changing of the Guard at Buckingham Palace and the annual Trooping the Colour are rituals and symbols of an enduring, albeit dented, monarchy.

The Halkin Hotel

WHEN A MAN IS TIRED OF LONDON, HE IS TIRED OF LIFE;

FOR THERE IS IN LONDON ALL THAT LIFE CAN AFFORD. Samuel Johnson

Room 506

London reeks of history. Small blue plaques affixed to many of its buildings commemorate the famous and the infamous, both real and invented, who lived in them; every step is where someone celebrated has gone before – from Charles Dickens to Sherlock Holmes. This is a metropolis with a very long and mixed record. The source and inspiration of much great writing and art, it is also home to a raft of museums and galleries. It seems that the city is itself a museum and full of them, from the eccentric Sir John Soane's House to the Victoria & Albert and the British Museum.

Green spaces are essential to relieve the urban crush. Hyde Park and St James Park are two that fulfil a function as 'the lungs of London'. Not far from either park, in the heart of Belgravia, is the Halkin Hotel. Sister to – perhaps the more elegant older sister – the much promoted and 'hip' Metropolitan Hotel, the Halkin is stylish in a discreet manner, modern but not of the moment. Its polished design is more for the long run. The traditional Neo-Renaissance exterior belies its modern Italian-designed interior, which is sleek and contemporary yet elegant and comfortable.

Each floor of the hotel has been named after and themed on a colour associated with a different element: water, air, fire, earth and sky. The fusion of Italy and the Orient (its owner Christina Ong is Singaporean) is evident in its design style. Subtle feng shui references are in the curves and circles used throughout the hotel.

A predominantly black and ivory interior has warmth added to it by rich wood veneers, and arched windows that let in the often bright London light. The hotel is favoured by fashion people, who will approve the staff clad in Armani uniforms and appreciate the black accents in the spacious rooms. The deep baths in the big marble bathrooms are perfect for a luxurious soak after a hard day of sight-seeing or business meetings. But just what you need to prepare yourself for an outstanding meal in the hotel's Michelin-starred Italian Restaurant overlooking a lush green private garden, a characteristic feature of London's inner elite areas.

Discreetly located – knowledgeable London taxi drivers will know it's off Grosvenor Place – in a quiet street, the Halkin is within walking distance of the shopping mecca of Knightsbridge, home to a host of name stores, streets and convenient for the museums of South Kensington. (The automatic spellchecker on my computer suggests the correct spelling of the hotel's name should be Halcyon; it certainly has that atmosphere.)

Bathroom of 506

The Lobby

FORGET SIX COUNTIES OVERHUNG WITH SMOKE,

FORGET THE SNORTING STEAM AND PISTON STROKE,

FORGET THE SPREADING OF THE HIDEOUS TOWN;

THINK RATHER OF THE PACK-HORSE ON THE DOWN,

AND DREAM OF LONDON, SMALL AND WHITE AND CLEAN,

THE CLEAR THAMES BORDERED BY ITS GARDENS GREEN. William Morris

The Halkin Hotel	Telephone: +44 207-333 1058
5 Halkin Street	
Belgravia	Facsimile: +44 207-333 1100
London SW1X 7DJ	
BRITAIN	E-mail: res@halkin.co.uk

The Melbourne city skyline from across the Yarra River

GRAND PRIX... POLE POSITION

Melbourne is the only Southern Hemisphere city on the Formula One car racing circuit. To the delight of many and annoyance of some, the track is close to the centre of the city, and the noise of the FI cars roars across town for three days. The Grand Prix, opening the motor-racing season's international calendar, is followed by the much quieter Wine and Food Festival.

Later in the year, more horsepower of a different kind fires up the city. The Melbourne Cup is Australia's take on England's Ascot Week, attracting racing enthusiasts and partygoers to see thoroughbreds gallop their stuff.

The Adelphi Hotel

THE ADELPHI HOTEL | Melbourne | Australia

These two major events add a sporty flavour to a city that has claimed to be the Australian capital of Arts and Culture. Nicknamed the 'Milan of the South Pacific', Melbourne is an urbane city once considered conservative, now called cosmopolitan.

Going off the deep end is not behaviour to be recommended at the Adelphi. This hotel, designed and owned by cutting-edge Australian architects Denton Corker Marshall, was their response to a self-set brief: to create a place that they themselves would want to stay in. For years the result, set in a refurbished 1930s building, was the only good hotel in an alternative contemporary style. Deliberately stark, in the heart of the central city, it is more like a club than a hotel.

One of its most remarked-on features is the literally over-the-top swimming pool. This is a glass-bottomed lap pool with a difference for it juts several metres beyond the edge of the hotel roof, giving swimmers a surreal view of the street below.

Kick too vigorously and you can send water spilling over onto the heads of unsuspecting passersby below, who are puzzled by a seemingly localised rain shower. There is a weird sense of suspension for the swimmer doing the Australian crawl out across the cantilevered edge.

The hotel's roof-top bar overlooks the pool, the twin-spired Cathedral, and across to the Edwardian dome of the Flinders Street Railway Station.

The Adelphi's furnishings are under the influence of the Memphis school of design to some degree. The bold clean design with bright colours and sharp edges has the architects' trademark oblique angles. Some of the sharp edges of tables have had shin protectors, affectionately called Avant Guards, fitted after a few guests claimed the furniture walked into them.

The minimalist bathrooms of granite and white translucent glass seem larger than they are due to maximum mirror.

All the furniture and rugs were designed by the architect-owners. They also designed the modernist entranceway to the city. Affectionately known to locals as the 'Big Zipper', this red and yellow sculpture protrudes over the motorway. Their predilection for cantileverage is evident on DCM's Melbourne Exhibition Centre as well, a distinctive building on the skyline.

Rooftop exterior

The Adelphi is right in the heart of Melbourne, a short walk to theatres, cinemas, restaurants, bars and shopping. Hairy Canary and the Gin Palace, bar-restaurants, are neighbours, in the same street. Langton's Restaurant and Wine Bar is in the next lane, a fortunate location.

Close by is the Southbank area, an elegant promenade alongside the Yarra River, complete with mega-casino, great cafés, bars and name fashion labels.

Melbourne is one of the few places left where trams are still a major mode of transport, and its City Circle tram circumnavigates the centre for effortless sightseeing.

The influence of the many immigrants who have settled in Melbourne is most obvious in the cosmopolitan cuisine on offer – from Italian to Vietnamese – and the world-class wines.

Melbourne is also a city with a sense of humour. Its Comedy Festival is one of the annual highlights in a action-packed calendar of events that lure more and more visitors there each year.

The pool over the edge

The Adelphi Hotel	Telephone: +61 3 9650 7555
187 Flinders Lane	
Melbourne	
Victoria 3000	Facsimile: +61 3 9650 2710
AUSTRALIA	

The Cardozo Hotel at twilight

HOT

HOT

HOT

SALSA CITY

The Cardozo Hotel looks like a sleek 1930s luxury liner moored on Ocean Drive. This masterpiece of streamlined design is a jewel among the many Art Deco gems on show in South Beach, part of the steamy tropical city of Miami.

Ocean Drive is a much-photographed streetscape of white and bright-coloured buildings pictured against the clear blue skies, aquamarine sea and lush palm trees of a town that is hot in winter, and hotter in summer. South Beach offers sun, sand, sensuality, salsa and sizzling heat, a potent cocktail that attracts visitors to what is often called the American Riviera and the sexiest city in the States.

Built in 1939 and one of many buildings designed by the prolific architect Henry Hohauser, the Cardozo was once a retirement home, as were other hotels in South Beach. Now Gloria and Emilio Estefan, the Cuban-born superstar singer and her award-winning songwriter-musician husband own it. Their business empire markets Cuban culture on the American mainland, and the informal headquarters of Estefan Enterprises is the hotel's patio restaurant.

With its white aerodynamic chairs, the Cardozo's beachfront lobby is reminiscent of a chic upper deck on a cruise ship. Just refitted, its original fireplace with marble mantel has been preserved, but in this climate it is for show rather than a necessity. The lobby's leopardskin patterned carpet is taken up for dancing to Latin bands on Thursday, Friday and Saturday nights, often until the sun comes up.

Reception with Marcus

You can perch on a high stool at the glamorous mirrored bar, or sit on the porch with a martini and watch the world go by.

Overlooking the ocean, the upstairs rooms respond to the tropical environment with shutters to close out the bright afternoon light for a siesta, old style planters' chairs to lounge about in and a languorous atmosphere redolent of sultry climes.

The Cardozo, and South Beach, market romance and relaxation, delivering on their promise in a winning package that combines Latino flair, a subtropical backdrop and retro style.

Most of the hotels along the South Beach streets were once cheap hotels put up during the Depression for working-class holidaymakers from New York. The developers had no money for size or rich decoration, resulting in an abundance of small hotels that rarely rise above three storeys. Architects drew inspiration from the aerodynamic design of planes, trains and automobiles, detailing their buildings with banding or racing stripes, cantilevered window shades and rounded corners admired by aficionados of the Art Deco style. But over a 40-year period, the hotels became low-rent housing filled with pensioners, until the Miami Design Preservation League, formed in 1976, determined to renovate the hotels. Miami Beach's transformation began, and from its once shabby state, South Beach developed an aura of chic.

The area has more than eight hundred examples of Art Deco, Streamline Moderne and Spanish Mediterranean Revival styles. The annual Art Deco weekend in the second week of January attracts half a million Deco fans from all over the world. While many of the Deco buildings have been preserved, or are in the process of restoration, some are not. One block back from the famed beachfront promenade are some that are a more sorry than pleasing sight. One is the Clinton Hotel, with a cracked façade and peeling paint. Its down-at-heel appearance is shared by several of its neighbours. However, the majority proudly parade in brightly painted colours in a role reversal that is a great American comeback.

The cost of renovation has been in the millions, but the payback has been much greater. Now no Art Deco period hotel can be torn down without approval, and if one is demolished, it must be rebuilt in keeping with the surrounding architecture.

There are other attractions too, including the mansion that belonged to fashion designer Gianni Versace, which is visited by tourist ghouls keen to photograph the steps on which he was shot dead.

Lobby with deco chairs

Bedroom of Room 302, overlooking the beach

Miami, and its communities like South Beach, is the promised land for immigrants, the recently displaced, and the recently retired, all seeking a better way of life or their time in the sun. Many Cuban exiles have established a beachhead here, close to their beloved country which itself is slowly becoming a tourist attraction.

A melting pot for many Hispanics, Miami's Little Havana neighbourhood emulates the sights, smells and sounds of Cuba. Tobacco stores sell hand-rolled cigars, *botanicas* offer herbal cures, men wearing guayabera (brightly patterned) shirts play dominoes, all this activity set to salsa and merengue music. Alluring aromas of Latin cuisine fill the air.

South Beach's attractions extend beyond architecture. The area has become a magnet for celebrities and fun lovers from all over the world, drawn to its cosmopolitan atmosphere, chic restaurants, pulsating clubs and white-sand beaches. Bronzed boys of all ages cruise the length of Ocean Drive in convertible cars with boom boxes thumping out music at full volume. Taut, tanned and terrific bodies lie on the beach, stroll or rollerblade along the streets. Regular thunderstorms on summer afternoons and early evenings seem to fit the predominantly Latino temperament of the place – flashes of lightning match the flashes of neon, often providing a double light show.

The feverish South Beach energy levels are at full pitch at night. All along the beachfront, it's party-time. Competing Latino bands play on every terrace, crowds promenade in the hot night air or sit at the many sidewalk cafes watching the constant parade of tourists and residents going by: the rollerbladers, models, wannabees, hunks... To help you stay awake and not miss what's going on, drink the strong black sweet coffee, Café Cubano.

Colourful and amusing lifeguard stations are dotted along the beach,
an architectural whimsy with appropriately hot colour schemes

THE NIGHTLIFE AND NEONS, THE SWELTERING HEAT

THE SUN WORSHIPPERS AND THE SALSA – IT'S A HEADY MIX.
THE URGE TO DANCE AND BE BRONZED IS HARD TO RESIST

The Cardozo Hotel	Telephone: +1 305 535 6500
1300 Ocean Drive	
Miami Beach	Facsimile: +1 305 532 3563
Florida 33139	
UNITED STATES OF AMERICA	www.southbeach.com

Diner in Deco style

New York skyline by day

HOTEL (THE MERCER) | New York | United States of America

MEGAPORTAL

Grand Central Station is one of the most famous entry points to the city of New York. This old style portal is the doorway to Manhattan for thousands who cross its concourse every day. Off to work, their heads down, few probably glance up at the heroic vaulted ceiling painted with constellations of the Zodiac.

The station's original turn-of-the-century splendour has been restored to better reflect its name.

To many, New York is the ultimate urban destination, the consummate city, home of skyscrapers and towers, night and day adrenalin, corporate success or failure, stardom or anonymity. Thousands of newcomers still arrive here with stars in their eyes, and as the song says, 'if you can make it there you can make it anywhere'.

One of Manhattan's older downtown neighbourhoods is SoHo, once the centre of the city's iron and steel manufacturing industry. The cast-iron buildings with huge windows and strong structures capable of supporting heavy loads were taken over by artists who set up loft studios here. They were followed by art galleries, restaurants and bars. Then the big-name retailers started to move in. Now SoHo's concentration of stores draws foreign tourists and local shoppers away from uptown's crowded streets.

The latest arrival on the block is the (Mercer) Hotel. Contradicting its desire for discretion, a delayed opening, the interior design and its celebrity guests have attracted attention and coverage. The hotel has achieved instant popularity in spite of itself. All the print material from stationery to matchboxes has the Mercer's name in parentheses.

'In small and exclusive hotels that tend to be used by celebrities, you want discretion and protection – from noise, phone calls, being photographed, even the city itself – and parentheses suggest that...' said the graphic designer Tibor Kalman. The theme continues on the bedroom doors, where the number is bracketed.

The Lobby tea bar and entrance to the Mercer's restaurant, 'The Kitchen'

The Mercer Hotel

The Reception

The Mercer building, constructed in 1890 for John Jacob Astor II, is detailed with Romanesque arched windows, cast-iron columns, vaulting and gargoyles. Its owner André Balazs, who also owns the legendary Hollywood hotel Château Marmont and the Sunset Beach Hotel on Shelter Island, didn't want something 'painfully stylish' for the new interiors. His vision was to provide an atmosphere of domestic bliss (one that you often have to leave home to achieve!). The much talked-about interior is by hot French designer Christian Liaigre, whose starting point was to think of the Mercer as a home, or maybe as a club for friends. 'I wanted to make it warm and livable – and calm; to get away from that SoHo people-in-black severity... that darkness which goes with the assault of New York, the noise, the aggressiveness.'

Accordingly, the lobby is more like a living room, with couches and armchairs covered in the Liaigre palette of chocolate, taupe, ivory and lilac. It can seat 100 people, considerably more than the normal living room. Tables and stools are made of luxurious dark African woods like wenge and ipe, a Liaigre trademark. One wall is lined with bookcases, filled with brightly coloured volumes on art, fashion, and design. So there is plenty to read while having a drink or waiting for friends. There is even a little room behind the bookcase to which you can retreat if you want solitude. This hotel caters to those who like and can afford informal luxury, perhaps the most expensive kind!

The glassed-off vestibule at the front is a bar and entrance to the basement level restaurant, the Mercer Kitchen. Balazs wanted a restaurant like 'a big eat-in kitchen, always the place with the warmest feeling and the best conversation,' so there are some communal tables as well. The food and service are excellent and not at all of the kind you usually find not always found at home!

This casual warm ambience has been meticulously planned. The atmosphere is slightly rarefied, the illusion of peace compared to the traffic noise outside a clever juxtaposition.

The rooms are serene, a welcome relief from the stress of the streets. Sunlight streams through arched windows, filtered by linen curtains. There is plenty of table space, as Liaigre believes that most hotels don't provide enough space to work or eat at. Generously proportioned full-length mirrors that lean against the wall also satisfy his concern for space. There is also somewhere to hide the shopping bags, with walk in wardrobe storage. SoHo provides ample opportunity for retail therapy, after which you have to lie down on a couch for some time.

The rooms have an air of simplicity rather than minimalism – less zen, more den. These are spaces to relax in as well as relaxing spaces, reflecting the sure yet light hand of this stylish designer. Liaigre believes that the purpose of design is to make you feel comfortable, and his trademark look is liveability.

The Lobby with floor-to-ceiling bookcase

Large bathrooms with enormous showers and marble king-sized bathtubs are based on studies suggesting that this is where most hotel guests spend around 70 per cent of their waking time. What they are doing for that amount of time was not revealed.

The Mercer has the aura of a sleek club, at the luxury end of the market in a city where hotel rooms are usually all premium priced. Its atmosphere is that of a super-chic home edged with a touch of attitude, which, for some, will make it even more authentic.

You could be tempted to move in and live here – although you might want to forgo the rubberneckers at the front door on the look-out for the famous. Unless you really are a name of course, in which case this might make it seem even more like home. Here you can wear your sunglasses at all times to avoid being recognised or disappointing the celebrity spotters.

Room (602)

The bathroom of (308)

New York by night

Directly across the street, the SoHo branch of the Guggenheim Museum lacks the distinctive architecture of its uptown parent or its Bilbao sibling. Instead it is cast in the same style as its neighbouring buildings, blending in, as the Mercer tries to do.

The hotel's instant popularity and the curiosity that engendered meant that the lobby was open only to guests and their guests. Obvious but tastefully attired security men bracketed each side of the plain black entrance door in the side street. They, not the parentheses, were fending off the voyeurs. Start spreading the news...

The Mercer	Telephone: +1 212 966 6060
147 Mercer Street	
New York	Facsimile: +1 212 965 3838
NY 10012	
UNITED STATES OF AMERICA	Internet: www.themercer.com

The Eiffel Tower – 986 feet/300 metres high

EURO STAR

Iron is what gave the City of Light its most famous landmark, the quintessential tower designed by Gustave Eiffel as the colossal centrepiece of the 1889 Exposition Universalle. This 'expressive mastery of iron' was praised as proof of French engineering superiority, and protested against as a threat to creative expression. One indignant French writer lunched at the Tower's restaurant every day, as it was the only place in Paris he could be sure of not seeing it. From the top, there is a marvellous vista, one that Parisians say only tourists pay to see, offering the visitor a dramatic perspective on this eternally romantic city.

HOTEL BUCI LATIN | Paris | France

Back down to earth, the pavements of Paris have been a perpetual lure for the millions of travellers who visit the monuments and museums and taste the food and wine of this most favoured city. Near one of the city's most stylish streets, the Boulevard St-Germain, is the Hôtel Buci Latin. This small post-modern hotel is in the heart of St-Germain-de-Prés, one of the elite *arrondissements* of Paris, just minutes from great shops, galleries, pâtisseries and restaurants, and a ten minute brisk walk to the Louvre and the Musée d'Orsay.

The Rue de Buci

The Hotel Buci Latin lobby

The neon sign is the first noticeable part of the hotel's frontage in a busy side street where the pavement traffic is such that it is quite easy to pass by it. Inside, the lobby announces that this is a quirky and stylish hotel. Warmly coloured in terracotta and yellow ochre, this is a cheerful reception with an eye-catching collection of art, furniture and the odd mini-racing car, that just happens to be there because Laurence Raymond, the owner, likes it. Downstairs from reception is the hotel coffee shop, full of interesting looking people and tempting cakes.

Take the tiny lift, typical of many Paris hotels, which means either you or your baggage go up to your room, not both. If you take the stairs, you will notice that the stairwell walls are covered in graffi, but on purpose rather than by tagger attack, to cheer up a traditionally dull transition space. More painting greets you when you arrive at your room, every door has been made an artwork by local artists. No chance of mistaking these non-standard entrances to the rooms, with your matching painted key. Inside, the rooms are more elegant than eccentric, in rich colours that add some extra drama to the excitement and pleasure that most people feel about being in Paris. Each is different, some on two levels, others with attic atmosphere bathrooms or a whirlpool for two on a private balcony.

This is a charming Parisian hotel, with a twist – a flair that is hard to describe but is there in the ambience.

The lobby may have a different look soon, as Laurence likes to update her hotel. But she will wait until she finds something that is right. The 'Go ahead, Make My Bed' sign took two years to devise, as an acceptable solution to having to provide guests with something to alert housekeeping; the reverse reads 'Shhh, I'm asleep or busy'.

The hotel is in the same street as a food market, illuminated with rows of white lights, and stocked with tempting food typical of Paris. In this star of European cities, one of the most-loved, most-visited and most-written-about of all, there is much to do see and discover. The Hôtel Buci Latin is an ideal base camp to set out from on your expedition.

Notice to Housekeeping

Hôtel Buci Latin	Telephone: + 33 1 43 29 07 20
34 Rue de Buci	
75006 Paris	
FRANCE	Facsimile: + 33 1 43 29 67 44

The ornate façade of the Grand Hotel Europa

CHECK-IN, CHECK OUT...

Since the collapse of the Iron Curtain, and the Velvet Revolution that led to the fall of the Communist government, Prague has been a popular travel destination on the European circuit. One of its main attractions is the exquisite core of eighteenth-century Baroque buildings that preserve the spirit of the Hapsburg Empire in the eighteenth and nineteenth centuries.

GRAND HOTEL EUROPA | Prague | Czech Republic

The lobby entrance

There is ample evidence that Prague is going global, with transnational labels such as Marks & Spencer and Benetton, and the ubiquitous American hamburger some of the clues that capitalism is effecting changes. But the city is full of signs to other times and cultures. Prague's most familiar monument is the medieval Charles Bridge, a pedestrian promenade for six hundred years, and home to souvenir sellers and artists. It spans the River Vltava, between the Mala Strana (Little Quarter) and the Old Town, and nearby is the Prague Castle. The buildings enclosed within the castle walls include a palace, churches, art gallery, the writer Franz Kafka's house and a monastery.

The ground-floor café

Mozart lived here while composing his opera *Don Giovanni*, and the piano he composed it at is displayed in the Mozart Museum. The Estates Theatre is where the opera was premiered in 1787. The Old Town Square is still the heart of Prague, and the winding cobbled streets and medieval arcades of the Old Town evoke the mysterious and dark world of the past. This is another city for wandering about, it is easy and intriguing to walk round, or alternatively to take a tram.

Wenceslas Square is home to many of Prague's Art Nouveau buildings. The Grand Hotel Europa is one of the more spectacular examples. Its statue-topped façade is painted and wrapped with hand-sculpted wrought-iron railings, and lettered in faded old gold. Seats on the ground-floor café's outdoor terrace are in demand for style and people watching but not for food or service, not the strong suit of this hotel. The first floor café is grandly fitted with chandeliers and hand-carved wood, but the service is as variable as the weather. The best rooms are the large and high ceilinged front-facing doubles. Some have balconies overlooking the square, the site of riots and revolutions in 1448, 1968 and 1989.

A hard to find example of modern Prague architecture is the Ginger and Fred Building, by Frank Gehry, one building that has two different parts, as did the famous dancing duo of Hollywood films. Apparently located on Rasinovo nabrezi, this Gehry landmark could not, or would not, be found by the taxi driver. It was tempting to crown him with more than the Czech coins.

A front-facing room

Grand Hotel Europa	Telephone: +420 2 2422 8117
Vaclavske namesti (Wenceslas Square) 25,	
Prague 1	Facsimile: +420 2 2422 4544
CZECH REPUBLIC	

Outside the Triton, with the cool Lawrence on door patrol

WWW.SFO.COM

The Blue Angels, aerobatic team of the United States Navy had come to town for the weekend. Celebrating Navy Week, the jets put on quite a show, and were they attracting attention. The noise was tremendous, and they seemed to be swooping so low over the city that we instinctively ducked as they roared overhead. No strident blue-winged creatures were at the door of the Triton Hotel, but there was a trident, held up by a figure of Triton, the mythical sea-deity whose aquamarine torso rises from the water at the entrance. The colourful exterior with its outdoor furniture is eccentric, but the lobby is truly extraordinary.

Even the bench seat looks puzzled, and the carpet is decidedly fishy. The columns are going for gold, the walls are trau-muralised and the Alice-in-Wonderland Caterpillar's chair appears quizzical. What can it all mean?

Its decorative oddness apart, the appeal of this hotel lies in its location, which is just a fortune cookie's throw from the Dragon Gate entrance to Chinatown, and only two blocks from Union Square, San Francisco's smart shopping precinct. (The Triton offers a Shoppers' Anonymous program that begins with a dry martini – sounds good to me.)

THE TRITON HOTEL | San Francisco | United States of America

The lobby with ottoman in pieces

BLUE ANGELS FLEW OVERHEAD,

DRAWING WHITE STREAKS ACROSS

THE SKY AS THEY SPED TOWARDS

THE SOUND BARRIER

Celebrity 'designers' have been invited to 'do their thing' devising the suites here, from Jerry Garcia of the Grateful Dead to hero guitarist Carlos Santana – who delegated the task to the designer of the band's album covers. Dolphins, whales and seals are given a permanent place in the suite by marine muralist Wyland. For environmentally sensitive guests, there are eco-rooms with ionised air and water filtration, hypoallergenic soaps and lotions, and energy-efficient lighting. 'Good-

A corner of the lobby for waiting jesters, with Cinderella's Coach on the table.

looking well-behaved pets' are welcome, at an additional charge. Alternatively, if you are not travelling with an animal, the Triton will provide a surrogate: there is a house duck, the Triton mascot, 'a shining example of polyurethane waterfowl reproduction' that is a web-footed feature of every room. The Triton duck is a much sought-after trophy. A new duck is hatched every year or so, drawing back past duckhunters to bag one. Next door is the hotel's bistro, Café de la Presse, with racks of newspapers from everywhere, and a stylish dining room – try the confit of duck: disconcertingly, it's a house speciality.

The TransAmerica Pyramid building has been described as one of the most instantly recognisable features of the San Francisco skyline, which has a plethora of visual tactile and edible interests. One of the very best-known sights of this city is its cable

Room 520, with Triton ducks out of water

The Vesuvio café-bar on Jack Kerouac Street, with the TransAmerica Pyramid.

car system, pulling the cars and their passengers up what are undoubtedly some of the steepest streets in the world, often with accompanying stunning perpendicular views of the Bay. A tip provided by the visitors' Quickguide, for travelling by cable car – 'if you miss your stop, wait for the next' – is practical advice that can in fact be extended to cover much of life. It's a little-known fact that the song 'I left My Heart in San Francisco' is actually a traditional roadsong for travellers – the ones who always leave something behind.

The Hotel Triton	Telephone: +1 415 394 0500
342 Grant Avenue	
San Francisco	Facsimile: +1 415 433 6611
California 94108	
UNITED STATES OF AMERICA	Internet: www.hotel-trtonsf.com

CLIFFHANGER

Clinging to vertiginous volcanic rock cliffs high above the caldera, is the village of Oia. The brilliant Aegean sun strikes its white roofs and blue domes, lighting a picture postcard view of the dramatic landscape.

Santorini is the southernmost island of the Greek Cyclades. Thousands of visitors, in the summer especially, flood here to visit this spectacular island, which legend suggests is home to the drowned ancient city of Atlantis.

Born of a volcano in prehistoric times, Santorini's ancient slopes were fractured by an immense eruption into multicoloured cliffs, black and ochre and tan, nearly a thousand feet high. Where there once was a mountain peak is now a caldera, the deep cavity in the summit of the extinct volcano, forming a cauldron for the sea. In the cliff face, sheltered from the strong north wind, people dug skafta, small rooms with barrel-vaulted ceilings. Earthquakes regularly shook the tiny villages, life was hard, and many left for Athens or the New Worlds of America and the Antipodes. In 1956 there were devastating earthquakes. One positive aftermath was that roads were built, and electricity installed. A new industry of tourism began. Now many ships cross the harbour, aircraft fly in daily and in the main town of Phira, cafés, shops and people crowd the streets. Discos and big hotels are down on the black sand beaches of Perissa and Kamari.

Perivolas Traditional Houses

On the northernmost tip of Santorini is the small picturesque town of Oia, built high on the rim of the caldera. A winding stairway connects it with the harbour far below, and its stepped paths lead through less crowded but still busy streets. On the edge of Oia is Perivolas, sixteen traditional houses, skafta converted from old wineries and stables into perfectly situated places to stay. The group of houses is family owned and strictly respects the traditional local character. Restoration of the houses has been under the supervision of a scholar of Santorinian architecture.

Each house is simply furnished in the Cycladic style, complemented with many antiques from all over the Aegean Islands. All are self-contained with spacious niches for beds, little kitchens, bathrooms with smoothed concrete floors, and hand-curved walls that are cool to the touch. Each is unique in its shape and character, and all have their own stone terrace. The houses step down to the bar and breakfast room, which opens onto a pool that curves over the edge of the cliff into the great panorama beyond.

The pool, the sea and the swimming man

Oia architecture

The view is simply astounding, almost confrontational, a dazzling vista of bluest sky and sea with dark red cliffs beyond. Watching the changing colours of this dramatic landscape as the day begins, through to the spectacular sunset that ends it, is a pleasure free to all who have eyes to see it.

The boundaries between the sea and the pool are blurred, a precipitous drop from the edge of one to the surface of the other. Houses and rock also blend together, and here on the terrace of this peaceful perch high above the caldera, with a glass or two of the crisp white Santorini wine, it is easy to forget that there is another world beyond.

Sunrise over Oia

Perivolas Traditional Houses	Telephone: + 30 286 71308
Oia-Santorini	Facsimile: + 30 286 71309
GREECE	E-mail: periv@santonet.gr

ORIENTATION

'Immortalised by writers and patronised by everyone,' said an anonymous journalist, about this classic hotel in the 1930s, when Singapore was known as the crossroads of the East and the Raffles label was seen on the steamer trunk of every seasoned traveller.

Built in 1887, it was declared a national monument by the Government a century later, and as can happen when governments take an interest in private property, it soon after closed down. However, this story has a happy ending, as the closure was for a major restoration. The hotel's first heydey was in 1915, and this date was used as the benchmark for returning Raffles to its elegant look of the times when sultans, statesmen, scribes and stars all tasted the colonial high life here.

The neo-renaissance façade of Raffles Hotel

The Sikh doorman

This 'White House' of Singapore, facing Beach Road and the South China Sea, is called after Sir Stamford Raffles, who founded modern Singapore in 1819. One of the few remaining great nineteenth-century hotels in Asia, Raffles has its own signature tune. The 1915 Raffles March was commissioned by the then proprietors of what was reported to be the 'most magnificent establishment of its kind East of Suez'. In addition, it has its own museum, a collection of travel memorabilia about itself, and its own drink, called the Singapore Sling, which is a complex concoction of gin, cherry brandy, cointreau, benedictine, pineapple juice, grenadine, and a dash of Angostura Bitters, more a fruit salad than a cocktail. An exotic taste, like the city of Singapore itself.

Orientation is, in zoological terms, the ability of animals to find their way back to a distant place, as in homing pigeons and migratory birds. Attracted to its history, I had stayed at Raffles a decade ago, definitely its shabby days. On my return, to see how it looked after its facelift, it had re-oriented itself to being a 'Grand Historic Hotel of the Far East'.

From the gleaming façade and the glamorous doorman to the resplendent lobby and lush gardens, this is a place transformed. All signs of shabbiness had been thoroughly dismissed, the hotel literally shone, every rough edge filed off and buffed to a gleam. This is a glittering comeback; a triumphant return after long and expensive cosmetic surgery with a new look that respects yet belies its real age. The original cast-iron portico that once sheltered the hotel entrance from tropical downpours yet was removed in 1919, has been reconstructed complete with the original stained glass.

The Lobby and its atrium attract crowds of visitors, so much so that it is closed mid-evening to all but the residents themselves. Each of the generously sized suites has its original fourteen-foot ceiling, arches and ceiling fans sustain the spacious airy atmosphere and light filters in through the verandah windows. Floors are teak, marble and tile, and the elegant period furnishings and oriental carpets add character. The old wooden and brass switch plates make an attractive feature of a necessary fitting. Although the feel of bygone days has been preserved, the rooms are not museum-like.

'Feed at Raffles when visiting Singapore' was Rudyard Kipling's advice many years ago, and still relevant. The Raffles Grill and the Tiffin Room with its famous speciality, tiffin curry, are renewed classic fixtures. The Writers' Bar – where

The Lobby and the original grand timber staircase

Suite 361

Bathroom of suite 361

novelists and travel writers such as Joseph Conrad, Somerset Maugham and Noël Coward made notes and conversation – still serves your choice of planters punch, as does the Long Bar, although this has moved location and changed substantially from its original incarnation. A hotel legend centres on the Bar & Billiard Room, where in 1902 the last tiger to be shot in Singapore met its demise, actually under the building, not, as a more fanciful story would have it, under the billiard table. Now there are other restaurants to feed at, the Raffles Hotel Arcade adjoining the original building has many more, the Empress Room with its Cantonese cuisine an elegant choice. Or you could leave the hotel's tropical garden surroundings of palm trees, ferns and orchids to walk literally just around the corner to the Imperial Herbal restaurant for a consultation with the herb doctor. You may be prescribed a variety of Chinese dishes and liquids to balance your yin with your yang. With luck one will be the delicious braised eggplant with pine nuts, but other dishes are as good. (Maybe not the deep-fried scorpions and crunchy black ants.)

The Somerset Maugham Suite

In front of the hotel are several Singapore white plumerias. Often planted around Asian temples, this tropical tree with its fragrant white flowers has been honoured by Buddhists for centuries as a symbol of immortality. The hardy plumeria is a continually flowering tree, a fitting match to the enduring legend that is Raffles.

Raffles Hotel	Telephone: +65 337 1886
1 Beach Road	Facsimile: +65 337 7650
SINGAPORE 0718	E-mail: raffles@pacific.net.sg

The view from Hotel Tresanton

I WILL MAKE A PALACE FIT FOR YOU AND ME
OF GREEN DAYS IN FORESTS AND BLUE DAYS AT SEA
Robert Louis Stevenson

COASTING

The Roseland Peninsula is on the warmer, calmer, southern side of Cornwall, a region that has extreme weather and rugged terrain, yet can be one of the mildest places in mainland Britain.

The Hotel Tresanton is moored here, once a yacht club, and then a hotel for yachtsmen, it is now owned, restored and reopened in its new rigging by Olga Polizzi, the sister of Rocco Forte. All the rooms, as well as the hotel terrace, have stunning sea views, looking out across the harbour to the St Anthony lighthouse. 'Tresanton' means the road to St Anthony, and en route by car you must pass through St Mawes. This is a seaside fishing village such as one expects to see in a film, a movie-set creation of a picture-postcard example that still seems undiscovered and unspoilt despite the summer-season crowds. Of course those who live and visit here have discovered it already. But in winter it can seem magically empty and atmospheric.

HOTEL TRESANTON　　　St Mawes　　　Britain

Hotel Tresanton is at the edge of the town, at the Castle end, a cluster of old houses on different levels built up the hill. It is blessed with a bewitching outlook, which could easily distract from the inner aspects. This is a hotel richly furnished yet simply fitted, with an attention to detail that reveals itself on close inspection. A sure hand has put this hotel together and made its interior prospect very pleasing to the eye.

This is a hotel with the atmosphere of a home, the lines between the two becoming blurred in an age of concern for and devotion to comfort. The Tresanton feels as though it is a private country house by the sea that takes in guests. Its large, comfortable sitting room reflects the character of its ownerswith a collection of furniture that seems to have evolved as it does at home, rather than having all arrived at once ready for opening day. A pleasing mix of old and new, there is plenty of plush settees and chairs to choose from if you have to share the room with others.

Each of the guestrooms is furnished differently with antiques and eclectic pieces, and all have a similar big view. The colours are soothing seaside-appropriate combinations, but fresh takes on that classic theme. Quietly luxurious, detail is understated but not overlooked in the deceptively simple rooms. There is space to move leisurely about, and in keeping with the coastal setting, the rooms are filled with the clear Cornish light.

The Tresanton has its own small cinema, an indulgence that seems preferable in every way to many other possible hotel offerings, such as health centres. Except that the cinema is only for use on rainy days – presumably there are some, as there are racks of rubberboots and umbrellas ready for such an event – and even these are attractively displayed.

A hotel by the sea should have a boat – here there is a fleet, from motorboats to a forty-eight foot classic racing yacht, the *Pinuccia*. Built to race for Italy in the 1939 World Cup, it is one of the sleekest and most timeless designs. Guests may charter the Pinuccia, with picnic and crew, to sail around the harbour.

The Sitting Room

The entrance to the restaurant

Dinner in the restaurant, with the chef that has been lured from London, where he trained with Marco Pierre White and the Roux brothers, gives the lie to any lingering doubts about provincial English cooking.

St Mawes Castle, built by Henry VIII in response to the Pope's threat to send a crusade against dissenting England, is just up the road. Behind and beside the hotel a beautiful little garden with a rare collection of subtropical and Mediterranean plants grows happily in this benign climate. A variety of other expeditions beckon further afield, such as to the Lost Gardens of Heligan – lost no more but the Found Gardens is less poetic – or to the Tate Gallery in St Ives.

With a cup of good coffee and a book, I was content to watch the sea and the land from my chair on the terrace. Surveying one of the greatest views in England, I felt as though I was on the upper deck, on the bridge of my own ship, and that a life on the ocean wave was the life for me. The restorative sea air is one very good reason to go south.

NOW, NATURE, AS I AM ONLY TOO WELL AWARE, HAS HER ENTHUSIASTS, BUT ON THE WHOLE, I AM NOT TO BE COUNTED AMONG THEM. TO PUT IT RATHER BLUNTLY, I AM NOT THE TYPE WHO WANTS TO GO BACK TO THE LAND; I AM THE TYPE WHO WANTS TO GO BACK TO THE HOTEL Fran Leibowitz

View of St Mawes from the Tresanton's terrace

How to get there: drive or train from London.

Hotel Tresanton St Mawes	Telephone: +44 136 270 055
Cornwall TR2 5DR BRITAIN	Facsimile: +44 136 270 053

WIZARD OF OZ

Sydney is blessed with one of the great natural harbours of the world. Set upon its waters are not one but two symbols synonymous with the city, the Harbour Bridge and the Opera House. Arching high over the water, the bridge provides an easy marker for the city's layout – northern Sydney is north of the bridge, southern Sydney is south of it, western starts immediately west, and so on. Affectionately called the Old Coathanger, the bridge was built for driving and walking across. Now those taking in the three-hour Bridgeclimb experience can scale the top of its high arch. With its back of curved 'spinnakers', the Opera House rises up from the water skirting it on three sides as though about to set sail. But it is permanently anchored here. Australia, the self-termed 'lucky country', is home to one of the world's most stunning buildings. It can be visited for theatre and opera performances, and to dine in its restaurants, or just admired from the air or by boat. And here in this water-centred city, you can also walk on water – at the Sydney Aquatic Centre, the main swimming pool floor may be raised for a cocktail receptions or conference dinners to create the effect of guests walking on water.

THE MEDUSA HOTEL | Sydney | Australia

Twin icons in Sydney's harbour

The Medusa Hotel

Host of the 2000 Olympic Games, Sydney already offers a marathon choice of sights and things to do. Just watching the city go by is one less strenuous option. Down in the Rocks area, the oldest part of Sydney, is the Museum of Contemporary Art. From its café terrace you can see the yellow harbour ferries go to and from their city base at Circular Quay; observe the people walking around this busy area and yes, look at the Opera House. Designed by Danish architect Jœn Utzon, its curved concrete, ceramic tiled, roof vaults have provided Sydney's waterfront with what has been aptly described as a 'sculptural ornament'.

Another ornamental building, on an inner-city street in fashionable Darlinghurst, is the Medusa Hotel. It has been described as 'a beautiful tall woman in a sexy red dress'. The grand Victorian terrace house is a heritage building now home to a small, stylish and quirky hotel, named after one of the three Gorgons in Greek mythology, Medusa, whose head, with snakes for hair, turned all who looked upon her into stone. This myth has inspired a poem, especially written for the hotel.

The reception with Medusa's portrait

The exterior's vibrant colour is continued inside, in a refreshingly innovative scheme that has touches of theatricality which are quite individual to each of the eighteen studio rooms. Some look onto the courtyard and the reflection pool, others overlook the streetscape and its passing parade. Lipstick pink carpet snakes up the stairs from the reception lobby, to spacious rooms with high ceilings and large windows. Some have a comfortable chaise-longue perfect for resting travel-weary bodies, great for a sore back and neck. The grand rooms are a mix of the traditional and contemporary, with cleverly inserted cubical bathrooms. While the Medusa only serves breakfast, a gourmet metropolis is on the doorstep. Close to the café culture, restaurants, nightlife and shopping of its location, the hotel is also in easy distance of other city attractions.

Room 206

Room 208

Sydney's sultry climate and pervasive beach culture is one of its many attractions. The Bondi Beach Festival of Sydney brings international acts in January, followed in February by the famous Mardi Gras, the gay and lesbian event of the year that everyone goes to. Great food is another attraction, in a city full of cafés and restaurants – Darley Street Thai and its offshoot Sailor's Thai, the Rockpool and the Wokpool, The Bank and the Vault, Tetsuya's, cars and food together at MG Garage and Fuel. Salt, the restaurant at the Kirketon Hotel, is just down the street from the Medusa.

In astronomical terms, Medusa's head is a cluster of small stars, including the bright star Algol, in the constellation Perseus. This definition seems better aligned to the Medusa's stellar position in Sydney's hotel planetary system.

And I knew such a man
(Whether in the body, or out of the body,
I cannot tell: God knoweth) –
2 Corinthians 12:3

It cannot be as some have claimed
That Medusa was ugly,
For men always turn away in disgust
From that which is repulsive.
She must have been extremely beautiful
To hold the gaze of men
And turn them, through wonder, to stone.
Her wild black hair, writhing like snakes,
Bewitched their sight, drawing forth their spirits,
And putting their souls outside their bodies.
The awesome power of the intellectual rage
That shot from her sloe-dark eyes held their gaze
In awe, and made their heads tremble from side to
Side. The glistening nectar beneath her tongue
(Dew to her lovely lips with their promise of moist
kisses) And her simple yet honeyed speech
Rung in their ears like the music of the sirens:
Now caressing, now bending their wills
To her determined purpose.
What wonder that men of great or feeble mind
Became statues to her wits and charms,
Mute witness and mirrors to her earthy glory!

PETER MARWICK

The courtyard

The Medusa Hotel	Telephone: +612 9331 1000
267 Darlinghurst Road	Facsimile: +612 9380 6901
Sydney	E-mail: info@medusa.com.au
AUSTRALIA 2010	Internet: www.medusa.com.au

The Lake Palace Hotel

It was here, to the heat, colour and noise of India that we came directly from the Ice Hotel, another white building set in a converse landscape and climate. While poles apart – one marble mirrored in a lake, the other ice frozen to the ground – there was still a striking similarity in their stand-alone positions and glittering physical presence.

A first visit to India is an assault on some timid western senses, the crowds of people pressing so close a shock, the beggars pathetic and unsettling and the demented traffic alarming. Our transit through Mumbai affected our nervous dispositions so much that we arrived in this comparatively quiet corner of India with an overwhelming sense of relief. This was tempered by the knowledge that at the Lake Palace Hotel we would be isolated and cocooned from real India.

Tea in the Amrit Sagar Bar

The hotel is set apart from that reality, and rightly or wrongly, we were glad to be within its calm and sheltering walls. But as we were to find out later in our journey, the real world is never far away. Viewed from the hotel's roof terrace, the romantic lake-side city of Udaipur in the Indian state of Rajasthan is both a beautiful and grand sight. The forts and battlements rear up behind the houses like cobras waiting to strike, but they stay still as their lake water reflection.

In the distance, crowds of women in bright-coloured saris come down to the shore to do their household washing, a sobering sight for one used to programming a machine to perform that function. Built on rock on a lake surrounded by hills in the mid-eighteenth century, the Lake Palace is shaped from pure white marble, from the domed chattris (pavilions), filigreed screens and carved columns, to the bottom of the swimming pool. Once the palace of Maharana Jagat Singh III (who built it so he could leave home and do what he liked without his father interfering) it is now a hotel mounded like rococco cake icing on four acres of rock.

Udaipur viewed from the Roof Terrace

The hotel has seven suites fit for modern day Maharana and Maharani. All are splendid, some astounding, with stained-glass windows, intricate inlays and carved silver headboards. Handknotted Kashmiri carpets, original Mewer miniature paintings, and rare antiques embellish the interiors of the hotel, making it a showplace for many of the Rajasthani arts and crafts. The guestrooms are much more demurely decorated than the suites and accordingly modestly priced, in comparison. As only guests may come aboard the Lake Palace, there is ample space to enjoy the gardens and terraces.

The Ajjan Niwas Suite

The Ajjan Niwas Suite

In a hotel full of real beauty, the Jharokha café is likely the most lovely of the many public spaces. Here and in the restaurant, the food was simply delicious.

The scarlet Royal Barge was restored by the production team on location here for the James Bond film *Octopussy*, working with Udaipur craftsmen who remembered the Gangaur boat as it was many years before. This is one of a fleet of twelve, but is by far the most spectacular. On special occasions and dinner cruises it is rowed grandly around the lake by the best-dressed oarsmen in the business who row with a stern countenance that can be somewhat disconcerting given the armour they sport. As we sat in the mid-afternoon sun by the lily pond, lazily writing postcards to friends and family, before we were due to leave for the airport, word came that our flight to Mumbai had been cancelled. There was no other scheduled from Udaipur that day, and there was not likely to be one tomorrow. The polite but harassed man at the hotel travel desk was sympathetic to our concern that we would miss our connecting flight that night to our next destination but his gentle shrug was eloquent in its helplessness. Suddenly a brick wall appeared and there behind it was the real world again. Fellow guests, Americans with Indian antecedents, who were in the same predicament, approached us with a plan.

Gangaur Boatmen

Five hours later we were passengers in a mad midnight chariot race with seemingly no rules, no lights and no traffic police. Driving through the black-ink night of rural India, a darkness occasionally punctuated with roadside campfires, in an Hindustani hirecar aimed by a driver seemingly possessed by speed demons, and a confrontational spirit that came to the fore every time a truck loomed in front of the headlights, was an adventure we wished we were not in. (The length of this sentence is nothing compared to how long the trip seemed to take.) Night driving on Indian roads can be an exhilarating experience, akin to playing Russian roulette. However, we completed our truck derby trial and arrived shaken but not stirred at a distant airport to resume our expedition, out of India.

The Gangaur Boat

Amused and emboldened by our adventurous departure, we have since determined to return to India, and to the Lake Palace Hotel. The old local saying, 'Pichola Ro Pani Pachho Gher Lave', meaning the waters of the Pichola lake will always call you back home is likely more a spell. Next time, we will have a less inflexible itinerary and make time to explore the many facets that make up India.

The Lake Palace Hotel Pichola Lake Udaipur 313001 INDIA	Telephone: + 91 294 527961- 73
	Facsimile: + 91 294 527974

The keyport of the Hotel Danieli

YET SOME THERE BE BY DUE STEPS ASPIRE

TO LAY THEIR JUST HANDS ON THAT GOLDEN KEY

THAT OPENS THE PALACE OF ETERNITY   John Milton

GRAND FINALE

These gold keys with their scarlet silk tassels open the door to the Byzantine charm of a fourteenth century Venetian palace; and by virtue of possession, entry to this mysterious 'studied, sly, enslaving' city.

HOTEL DANIELI | Venice | Italy

The front door of the Hotel Danieli

Arriving in Venice for a second visit, I am struck by the same feeling of slight unease. It is an almost physical alertness to something not quite right, some out-of-kilter nervous response. My self-diagnosis is that I am experiencing the Looking Glass effect, crossing, like Alice through a mirror, into the myriad paintings and sketches depicting Venice which I have absorbed over the years. That sense of dislocation, the contemporary inserted into an historical envelope, is disconcerting until the familiar signs of modern life direct a return to reality.

My first visit was ten years ago, in winter, when the shopkeepers open for business greeted me with mild surprise. Like migratory birds, tourists were expected with the warmer weather. Now, more and more people winter in Venice to avoid the summer crowds. But this is a city invaded daily, weekly and monthly by the hordes seeking to discover the legend for themselves. As a result, there are few moments when you have Venice to yourself: perhaps on an early morning when, glimpsed from a gondola or water-taxi, the city floats mirage-like on quiet waters; or at sunset as day-trippers retreat from the cluster of islands and the palace of the doges is flushed a deeper pink. Inhabitants appear ambivalent about the invasion of their city, but while tourism is their livelihood, Venice is in danger of being trampled into the lagoon's quiet waters.

THE MERE USE OF ONE'S EYES IN VENICE
IS HAPPINESS ENOUGH. Henry James

The distinctive terracotta façade of the Hotel Danieli and winter gondolas

The Golden staircase

The Hall Dandolo

The Hotel Danieli's terracotta-and-white arched façade has been a Venetian landmark for six hundred years. Entering the enveloping front doors is another step back in time. The interiors probably looked very much the same when guests stayed centuries ago, although modern amenities have been added.

The palace was once the home of Venetian nobles, the Dandolo family. One of its most famous sons, Enrico Dandolo conquered Constantinople in 1205, and brought back gold, marble and other treasures with him, including four horses. These now-famous bronze animals stand above the entry of the Basilica di San Marco in Venice's busiest square.

The Danieli's lobby opens onto a magnificent atrium, with a grand staircase of gold marble leading up to the suites and guest rooms, all furnished in Empire style with precious antique pieces. The most opulent of these is the princely Doge's Suite.

Hung with chandeliers crafted on Murano, the island centre of the Venetian glass-making industry, the Hall Dandolo is a splendid setting for the simple ritual of afternoon tea, which may seem too prosaic an activity in this soaring poetic space.

A city of more than a hundred and eighteen islands, linked by a labyrinthine fretwork of footbridges and canals, Venice was once a mighty maritime nation. Every Ascension Day, to symbolise the marriage between city and sea, the doge would sail his golden barge from the lagoon to cast a wedding ring into the Adriatic, symbolising the marriage of Venice to the sea. This seven-hundred-year-old ritual is re-enacted on the Grand Canal each September with a regatta of richly decorated patrician gondolas.

Although its grandeur has faded, Venice continues to reign, if only over the imaginations of those drawn to her colourful and prosperous past.

Last frame – the view of the lagoon and the Church of Santa Maria della Salute from the terrace

Hotel Danieli	Telephone: +39 41 52226480
Riva degli Schiavoni, 4196	
30122 Venice	Facsimile: +39 41 5200208
ITALY	

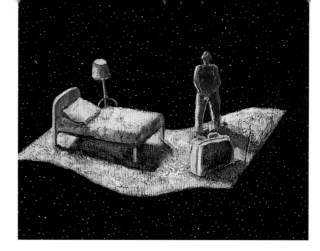

WHERE TO NEXT?

The world of the modern nomad is becoming smaller.

Out of this world may be the next border to cross, to boldly go where few men and even fewer women have gone... into space. There, places to stay may be what you are wearing when you arrive, carrying your own capsule instead of a suitcase – special travel clothes that provide your cocoon, far from home. No gravity means weightless suitcases, a definite improvement.

ALL ANY OF US NEED IS A VERY LIGHT SUITCASE Oswald Wynd

Soon, taking the shuttle could mean more than transport to and from the airport. Shuttle spacecraft, lunar sightseeing trips and orbiting space resorts are already in planning by extra-terrestrial travel agents, for those able to afford the astronomic airfares.

Travelling will be down on earth for a while yet. Hotels here will continue to become more like home, as they strive to customise and personalise the travel experience for their guests. Soon you will be able to go straight to your room without checking in, your credit card, fingerprint or even your retina will become the 'key' that opens the door. When you do, the hotel computer will register your arrival. Rooms that remember your preferences, interactive so you can create your preferred surroundings and own sleeping experience, will be available. Invisible hotel staff, multipurpose furniture – beds that cure jet lag, adjust from hard to soft, disappear into the wall – and luggage that is programmed to follow you, obediently to heel, are all in the realm of possibility.

Whatever, wherever, there'll still be places to see and people in search of adventure. Travellers often start planning their next journey on the way home from the present one. We are planning ours now.

NO MATTER WHERE YOU GO – THERE YOU ARE Earl MacRauch